Raising

The Inner Child

Discover Your Unique Path to Healing

Simi Ahuja, MD

Raising The Inner Child:
Discover Your Unique Path to Healing

Copyright © 2024 by Simi Ahuja, MD

For more about this author please visit www.drsimisays.com

Library of Congress Control Number: 2024941861

Paperback ISBN: 978-1-965092-00-2
Hardcover ISBN: 978-1-965092-01-9

1. Main category—BODY, MIND & SPIRIT / Inspiration & Personal Growth
2. Other category—BIOGRAPHY & AUTOBIOGRAPHY / Memoirs
3. Other category—PSYCHOLOGY / Emotions

First Edition

It is with deep gratitude that I dedicate this book to my mom and dad. Thank you for the gift of life and your support so that I could unravel the entangled energies that have existed between us for lifetimes; so that we can all attain moksha.

I would also like to dedicate this book to both of my daughters, whose souls have chosen to walk this difficult path with me. They have gone through many challenges in their short lives.

Your support through my journey means more than I can say, especially considering the hardships during your tender years, years that should've been filled with the gentle embrace of a loving home, but instead were clouded by worries about your mother's inner struggles and whether she would ever make it out of the morass in her psyche.

With much Love and gratitude

Table of Contents

Introduction 1

Chapter 1: A Sovereign's Way 4

Chapter 2: The Straw That Began My Awakening 12

Chapter 3: The Mystical Healer 32

Chapter 4: Russian Dolls 54

Chapter 5: The Karmic Predicament 75

Chapter 6: Secure Attachment with Yourself 93

Chapter 7: Doing the Work 109

Chapter 8: Let the Preparations Begin 124

Chapter 9: Jumpstart Your
Healing Journey Now 144

Chapter 10: Yoga of Relationships 161

Epilogue 172

About the Author 175

Introduction

THIS BOOK HAS BEEN A long time in the making. A journey over lifetimes has culminated in this book. It is a journey that will move you through the train of time. As you sit in this train, you will have a window seat. You will feel the chugging of the train as it transports you through one lifetime to the next, slowing down in between to give you a glimpse of the important moments. Moments that shaped me. Moments that spoke the loudest. Moments that deserve to be heard. Moments that needed to be unraveled.

Each momentary stop has its own unique flavor, imbuing your own senses, daring them to awaken. Each moment has its own unique fervor, awakening your own feelings, lingering on each moment just long enough for you to savor the exotic umami dance of life and Karma brought into awareness by the courtesy of the inner child work.

The distance is long and covered with thoughtful timelapse, not speeding up so much that the important moments are missed. You can travel right alongside me into the darkness of our collective psyche. I will be your personal guide to the exploration of the deep caverns of the mind. Perhaps you can find the courage to shine a light on your own personal psyche by connecting with your inner child. I am offering classes on Raising the inner child so you can learn to strengthen your connection with your inner child. Each moment I reveal is being unraveled to show you the nooks and crannies of the collective mind. Your inner child will open the portal into your personal mind. Together we will inquire, investigate, and extricate ourselves out of the deep tunnels of the mind and find the source of light.

All I did was go on this train ride alone. It seemed dark and terrifying at first. Like a horror movie. A living horror movie, nonetheless. A dynamic horror movie, where nothing remained the same. The scenes were ever-evolving, and the stage was ever-revolving. All in the blink of an eye.

The cast was always the same, but the characters were different.

The deeper I went into the time continuum, the more light I found. What I found was so magical that it left me disillusioned about my 3D physical reality. It lifted the veil of the ego, catapulting me into a different dimension in this time-space continuum.

I saw that things are not as they seem. Things are not what your senses would have you believe. Things are not what your mind would have you think. I am not who I thought I was. I am also not *what* I thought I was.

As someone who has been denuded of everything, I am confident I can help you to navigate the tunnels of darkness. I have returned to take you with me on this mysterious journey into the mind and the innermost workings of the universe. Will you dare to step on this time train with me to explore the untamed wilderness of the mind?

What do you have to gain? The gains are as unfathomable as the journey is deep. It will expand your mind. It will open your heart. It will evolve your soul. It will bring you back home to you.

I warn you that it is not without drama. All the drama that the Karma produced in my life is written for your contemplation. For you to pick through.

You can use your own discernment. Use this ride as an inspiration or entertainment. Neither one is wrong. Both sides are right for you are GOD in drag. How you choose to view the ride is at your will. Thy will be done by the God that lies within you. May the journey begin *chug-a-chug-a-chug*.

Chapter 1

A Sovereign's Way

I WOULD LIKE TO PREPARE YOU mentally from the outset by saying that this book will challenge you. It is my intention to make you question all that you believe. I questioned everything I was taught as a child born into a Sikh family, and so should you. Because we should not take up a belief in something that we have not experienced. The moment we take up a belief of another is the moment we give our power away. Because we live in a magical universe, we create what we believe. Your reality does not have to be the reality of your fellow human beings. You have the power to create a different world for yourself than the one your neighbor creates.

The power to explore the deeper truths within the universe is contained within you. You just need the courage to embark upon the journey within. To do that you have to be willing to set aside your current beliefs to search for the truth. Put those beliefs aside for a moment so that you are not biased as you embark upon this journey. Until you have *realized* the universal truths for yourself, I recommend reserving your judgments. If you have not walked this path, and you judge, those judgments will be erroneous, and erroneous judgments create suffering and Karma.

The concepts that I speak about are my own realizations. They may trigger you, and that is okay. The trigger simply means that there is an erroneous belief in your psyche that is being shaken up. Shaking up our beliefs, especially foundational beliefs, requires a trigger. It's the shaking up that allows them not to have such a tight hold on us. Notice what your triggers are instead of reacting to them. Ask yourself, "Why am I triggered?" Then hold still and listen for the answer without getting in the way. Without having preconceived notions of what it may or may not look like. Your trigger will point the way to your healing, if you have the ears to hear.

The concepts presented in this book are different than concepts you may have read about in any other book because my perception of the world has shifted since I began this journey in 2008. It doesn't mean that we crucify the person who thinks differently than us or who is presenting new ideas with a shift in paradigm of how we think. It is revolution in our thinking that is in the making; don't be so quick to cast the first stones. As Jesus said, "Whichever one of you has committed no sin may throw the first stone…" We have all done things that we are not proud of and may not even be aware of. The cog wheels of the universe turn with the force of Karma. It will behoove you to walk this path before casting a stone of judgment.

I have come to the conclusion that all religions speak the same language and have the same teachings. It's the authorities that have falsified the teachings to meet their agendas, whatever they may be. I, personally, have no faith in the authorities who run religions and hence have the ability to control the masses to meet their egotistical needs.

I have attended churches of Christ-based religions. Each time I have heard them talk about how Jesus died for our sins. I personally don't agree with this particular teaching, but I am willing to go along with it for the sake of argument. But why do they stop there? Jesus also said that "You too can do what I can do and more." Why are we not taught the "more" part? Because all of us have the power to create miracles. Why doesn't anyone talk about that? What are they hiding? I don't know about you, but I cannot trust anyone who has ulterior motives. I truly believe that my life was orchestrated on my behalf by God himself so I could be empowered by the knowledge about the truth behind the illusory world.

As a Sikh I was taught that ours is the best religion in the world. Sikhism is only 500 years old. So, do you mean to tell me that everyone who lived prior to the evolution of Sikhism is doomed? And everyone who doesn't tie a turban or cut their hair is condemned to hell for eternity? That they can never commune with God? Such nonsensical teachings do not serve to unite. They serve to divide. As for me, teachings such as this drive me to go within and go in search of the truth for myself rather than put my blind faith in the supposed teachings delivered by a flawed human.

Whether it's Sikhism, Hinduism, Christianity, Catholicism, Jainism, or Buddhism, I declare that I will not be suppressed by any authority who is telling me what to believe and what not to believe. For I am created by God in His likeness. Nothing and no one else has authority over me. I will not be enslaved by anyone by catering to their fabricated beliefs constructed to subjugate humanity. You can choose as you wish.

I believe that I have been given this body by God, and this body is my sacred temple. It is my sanctuary. I don't need churches or temples to tell me how to have a relationship with God. All I have to do is go within to convene with God. My relationship with God is a personal matter, and *no one* gets to have a say in it. I don't need to go to a Sikh temple or drink the blood of Christ to be liberated even though his teachings, along with Buddha's teachings, have shaped me in many ways. Their teachings are the way leading me to the concept of "Buddha mind, Christ consciousness." If I have a question, I will take it up with God himself. I don't need a middleman such as a priest, a minister, or a rabbi to delegate what transpires between me and God, because they are humans and can and do and will make mistakes. I don't want their mistake to cost me my liberation. I am very protective of my liberation.

In this book I will take you on my journey. As you embark upon this journey with me, you will notice that you may be feeling confused, frustrated, and a whole host of other emotions. It is my intention for you to feel those emotions as you travel alongside me in your imagination, so that you can get a glimpse of what it is like to be me; to live in a state of confusion as someone who was abused, as someone whose psyche was severely wounded. It wasn't until I went in search of the truth that I gained clarity.

I was born and raised in New Delhi, India. Going to Gurdwara was a daily ritual, along with the physical, emotional, mental, and sexual abuse. Migrating to the states from India with my family at the ripe age of twelve threw me into a whirlwind of identity crisis. Questions such as, "Does reincarnation really exist?" began to gnaw at me. "Was all that I learned as a Sikh, wrong?" "Is it only Christians who will be saved? Or is it only the Sikhs who will be saved?" "What about all the other religions? Are they all doomed?" I wanted to find out the truth for myself because I didn't know who to believe. How can there be such a big difference in the fundamental principles of the universe? My quest for truth behind the internal knowledge and wisdom drove me to embark upon a journey into self-discovery, with my biggest question being, "Who am I?"

As a twelve-year-old, I began to question everything in life. I didn't know who or what to believe. This made it extremely difficult to live life. I didn't go to church and no longer knew whether to go to a Sikh temple. As an adult and as a mother, I didn't know what to teach my kids. What kind of a foundation can I help them to set so that they don't feel so lost in life? How do I counsel patients with end-of-life issues as a doctor? How can I console them? And the list went on.

I remained in a state of confusion until almost thirty years later, when I met my spiritual mentors, who have since guided my path toward the universal truths. They didn't tell me the truths but rather sent me on a journey where I could discover them for myself. This way I could not be fooled by anyone who tried to bamboozle me, such as the so-called religious scriptures that claim to know the truths behind the mysteries of the universe. This way I could hold steadfast in my experience of the universe.

The only way to know these deeper truths is by going on a journey yourself. Don't take my word for it. The invitation is to go within and get the answers for yourself, so there is no mistaking the truth. Inner child work became the train upon which I was led to the exotic places in the universe. It taught me that the universe is within me. All I have to do is have the eyes to see and ears to hear these truths. Which meant keeping an open mind no matter what was presenting itself to me. Therein lies the challenge of this journey, because we are conditioned by certain religious beliefs during our upbringing. We are taught certain societal norms, deviation from which will subject you to isolation whether in the way of verbal, physical, or psychological abuse. Whether in the way of expulsion from society or exile into psych wards or correctional institutes. Society will beat you into compliance one way or another.

With blind leading the blind, how far do you think we can go? After all, Jesus was exiled from the world by way of crucifixion.

The process of inner child work is deep and rich with wisdom. Its depth is unfathomable, and its wisdom is inexhaustible. I cannot even begin to teach you what it has taught me. But I can share some examples and outline what I did so you can embark upon this journey for yourself. I have chosen to share some very personal stories in hopes of illiciting the knowledge I received from the inner child work. It is a living breathing process. It is dynamic, not static.

I don't know when I became like the leaf in the wind and allowed it to take me where it wanted to take me. The inner child work became the wind that carried me with precision. It took profound trust and complete surrender for me to do this work and go to the depths that I have gone to.

When I first embarked upon this journey, I cast aside all that I had been taught up until that point, except for one thing. This thing resonated deeply within me, and I knew it to be true beyond the shadow of a doubt. It served as a foundation upon which I could build. As a Sikh, I was taught that God is within me. This became the basic premise for my journey. I wanted to go in search of the God within me. I began to search for a teacher who could teach me the art of looking within. Who could help me to find God within.

We, as humans, have strayed so far from consciousness that we have forgotten who we are. We have forgotten that we are divine beings. Through sharing my experiences on this journey, it is my intention to give you a reference as to what this journey can do for you if you allow it. Your journey will be unique to you. I hope that after reading mine you won't think you have gone crazy and that you will have the courage to persist.

This journey will help you to remember who you are at your core. You are not your body. You are not your ego. You are a soul. But we think we are the body, and we are the ego. I have used inner child work to help me to realize that I am a soul. The inner child work has helped chisel away at my soul so that I could claim my divinity from the body and the ego. My experience has taught me that we incarnate for the evolution of the soul. A soul's growth cannot happen when we are not willing to go past the comfort zone. No one has learned something new by staying comfortable.

Since there is so much conflict between one religion's teachings to another, I knew I had to let go of all that I had learned and start fresh. I began by reading books such as *A New Earth*. I also read *Disappearance of the Universe* and became a "Course in Miracles" student, during which I learned about the teachings of Jesus and Buddha. While I did not want to subscribe to any religion, I was inspired by the teachings of Jesus and Buddha and wanted to be like them. Some of their teachings resonated deeply within my soul. At this point in time, I had shunned most of the teachings of Sikh gurus, thinking they didn't know much. I also didn't want to subscribe to *all* of the so-called teachings of Christ and Buddha. I wanted to pick and choose. I stuck with the teachings that pointed the way inward. If they didn't point the way within, I objected to being a student of those teachings. I had set some basic principles for myself that I followed throughout my journey.

I was glad to have met my spiritual mentors, for they pointed the way within. They showed me that the deeper truths behind religions are the same, but it's the authorities who have lied to the masses to create confusion. I realized that there were more commonalities between Sikhism and Christianity than I thought. I was already familiar with the commonalties among other religions, such as Hinduism, Islam, and Jainism. I also realized that universal truths are the universal truths no matter what the religion. The universal truths are not bound by religions. The leaders of religions are also human beings and can disperse misinformation whether intentionally or unintentionally. It is up to each individual to go in search of the universal truths for themselves, yet so few of us do. More often than not, most of us end up chasing things that bring no real meaning to our lives.

It is my invitation to keep an open mind throughout this book. This will help you to learn the principles that I want to bring attention to, because the inner child work has the power to clear your Karma and liberate you from the cycle of death and rebirth. Or as Christians would say, it has the power to "save" you.

As I said earlier, the concepts I present in this book are uncomfortable and challenging. This is why is important to read with your heart rather than your mind. I have learned a lot on this journey, and one of the key concepts is that only the truth has the power to both free you and trigger you. Nothing has the power to unravel your energy like truth does. And nothing else has the power to trigger you like truth does. If you feel triggered at any point in time, I invite you to take a step back to see the truth behind the concept. We can only grow through discomfort.

"A person's success in life can usually be measured by the number of uncomfortable conversations he or she is willing to have."

—Tim Ferris

Chapter 2

The Straw That Began My Awakening

THE YEAR WAS 2008, AND the housing market was crashing. My husband and I had taken cash advances from credit cards in his friend's name and had bought land in India. Little did he realize that even if we used his friend's credit cards, we would still have to make minimum payments. Our minimum monthly payments were more than my one month's salary and a locum position, even on my medical doctor's earnings. This did not include groceries or any other household expenses for us, including my two young daughters. We couldn't sell the land in India owing to the market crash, as the value had dropped, nor could I make payments as there were so many. He would continue to apply for new cards that were offering zero percent interest so he could juggle the cards. It was all making my head spin.

I remember one summer my then-husband was in India making his quarterly trip when he called me. He felt entitled to live like a king, being a stay-at-home dad while being married to a doctor. It gave his self-esteem a boost to be able to travel on a whim, leaving the responsibility of taking care of our two girls to me. Along with caring for our girls while he was away, I worked two jobs to support his shopping habits. I was the dutiful Indian wife, after all. I had been trained well by my culture and family to *obey*.

I had just parked my car in the parking lot of the small grocery store in town. I heard his voice on the other end, "Can you call the credit card company and get a $5,000 cash advance?" My heart sank, as if the floor had been pulled out from under me. "I don't think that's a good idea," I replied, while knowing nothing I said would be taken into account. "Joo always say no to anything I am about to do," he said. Hearing my hesitation, he went on to say, "Behind every successful man is a vomen, and joo pull me back all the time. This property that I am going to buy vill be vorth a lot of money one day. But joo alvays hold me bac. Becoz joo always say no that things never turn out the vay I vant them to. This is vhy ve never make money. This is vhy ve are broke all the time."

He had me exactly where he wanted me. I felt guilty for saying no because I felt responsible for our financial situation. I blamed myself for not making enough money. I felt guilty for not being the woman that he wanted me to be. I felt guilty about not supporting him more than I was. I mean—I was working two jobs; I was also taking care of all the household chores the best I could even though he was a stay-at-home dad. I was helping my kids with their homework as I was more educated than he was. *But perhaps I could do more to support him*, I thought.

What if he was right? What if we could make tons of money off the properties in India? I felt helpless and didn't know what to do as my salary was already going toward minimum payments. We were in so much debt that it would be nice to make some easy money and pay off the enormous amount of debt that we had already accumulated without my having to work two jobs. Eventually, I gave in without much of a fight. I agreed to call even though I had an uneasy feeling that it was likely not a good idea. I hung up the phone with my husband and with a heavy heart, feeling lost and confused, I got my credit card out of my purse and called the number on the back. I asked them for a $5,000 cash amount, which the gentleman on the other end was more than happy to transfer over to my bank account. I called my husband back to let him know that the cash was in our bank account. He expressed his gratitude for supporting him and told me what a good wife I was. He also thanked me for not getting in his way.

I hung up the phone and sat in the parking lot reflecting on what had just happened. What was wrong with me? Why did I not want to support my husband? Was I really a bad person? Why couldn't I be that woman who could make him a successful man? Why did I always hold him back?

I thought about all the other debt that we had accumulated over the years. Some was under my husband's friends' names that he had signed for. He had coaxed them into giving him their Social Security numbers so he could open up credit cards under their names and told them it was so that he could help them build their credit, as they had just migrated from India. He, of course, always promised to pay off the credit cards. What he hadn't realized was that the banks did not want to give him any more cards because they knew how much I made and how many monthly payments we could reasonably handle. These people are not stupid. They do their math! That is what got us here.

This was not the first time he had asked me to do something like this. I couldn't say no to him. I had just completed residency in Family Medicine and had landed a nice six-figure job. Yet we couldn't make ends meet. Being an MD, I should not have to struggle with my finances. Why was I struggling so much? Where did I go wrong?

If it was just my financial life that was messed up, I don't think I would have gone digging for whatever it was that was wrong in my life. But my personal life was also in shambles. My younger daughter was about two years old, and my older one was about nine. I was still a resident, and my father-in-law was visiting us from India.

Wearing my light blue scrubs, hair tied up in a bun, I entered our two-bedroom spacious apartment. I had just gotten off from being on call and had been gone for about thirty-six hours. I came home and saw my father-in-law and my husband sitting in the living room. I put my bag down by the door and went straight into the kitchen hoping there would be something for me to eat.

As I looked in the fridge there was nothing to eat, not even a crumb. I asked my husband what the girls had eaten over the past day since I was gone. He said, "I just fed them some frozen food. And now ve vere just vaiting for you to get home and cook." My jaw dropped, in my mind. I could not believe the words that came out of his mouth! Did he just ask me to cook after I spent thirty-six hours on call, and he was the stay-at-home dad? I was horrified that he would even say something like that. On top of that he went on to say how I was over-reacting. After all, it is an Indian wife's duty to take care of her family.

He saw nothing wrong with the situation. In fact, he felt I was the one in the wrong. That I should be able to come home and cook and clean for the family after work. That I should take care of my father-in-law, who was visiting us from India. That would be the respectful thing to do. And I needed to be that dutiful wife so he could look good as the oldest son in the family. Never mind that I was going through the stress of residency. But I always put him first, always questioned myself. Always doubted myself as to whether or not I was doing the right thing. *There must be something wrong with me*, I thought.

Something felt off. But I didn't know what. How could I even begin to sort out who was right and who wasn't? I often blamed myself for not having a typical Indian woman's desire to take care of my in-laws. I often felt guilty for not wanting to take care of them and wondered what was wrong with me. This was why I knew that I would never have a successful arranged marriage. Hence, I married for Love, or what I thought was love. I felt that I would disgrace my family if I went through with an arranged marriage because there are certain expectations from the boy's side of the family regarding what the girl would do when she married into the family. I knew that I didn't want to do all the cooking and cleaning and taking care of my in-laws in the manner that would be expected of me. I thought marriage for Love would be better and would give me some liberation without getting my parents involved. It sounded good in my head. But I didn't realize the guy I had married had the same traditional expectations even though he'd told me he didn't.

This battle between my desires and cultural expectation to be a good girl was an old one. Sitting in that parking lot, a lot of random thoughts about my childhood came flooding back. Reflecting on when we lived in India, I remember thinking that I would not be a submissive wife. I saw how my mother was treated by her in-laws. "Your mother has big boobs. She is not as pretty as your father. I don't know why your father married her," said my dad's sister. I don't know what she had against my mother. After all, theirs was an arranged marriage.

If she did not want her brother to be arranged with my mother, why didn't she say something when they were getting married? I thought.

Then I began to think about how I had wanted to be independent ever since I could remember. I was about nine years old, and my family and I were visiting my mom's sister in Punjab, India. My mom's cousin had come over, and I found out that he knew how to read palms. I eagerly put my left hand out and asked him to give me a reading. "What do you want to know?" he asked.

"Will I have a house of my own?" I asked in Punjabi.

He took my hand and started to look at it. Then after a few seconds of careful thought he said, "Yes."

"No, I mean with my own money," I clarified.

"Yes, you will have a house that you will buy with your own money," he said, smiling.

There must've been something magical about the parking lot because I also remembered that even when I secretly started dating my husband, I had told him that I did not want to be a typical Indian wife. At the time he had agreed that I would not have to take care of his parents. He said that he understood that I wanted to go to medical school. He pretended to be someone he was not, and I bought into his lies like a suggestible fool.

I thought about that day when he told me he expected me to cook after coming home from a long, grueling thirty-six-hour shift, during which I was critiqued every minute of the day; I felt betrayed by him. I felt like he had tricked me into marrying him with lies. He thought he could change me after we were married. So, it didn't really matter what I wanted.

He told me that his dad always said, "A woman is equal to a man's shoe and should know her place." This was after we had been married for nine years! Well, that's not what he had said when we were dating. Was that all a facade? Was our marriage a lie? I was hurt by what he'd said. He wasn't the man I had met; had he hidden his true feelings? I didn't know what to believe anymore. Perhaps I didn't want to face the truth that I had been lied to for the entirety of my marriage. That I left my family for this facade of a "marriage."

My whole life suddenly felt like it was a lie. A lie that I could not face before that moment in the parking lot. How could I have taken such a step in haste so as to desert my family for a man who did nothing but lie to me to fulfill his own agendas.

Nothing in my life was working out. My health was also beginning to suffer as I was diagnosed with prediabetes. What on earth was happening? What was going on? High amounts of minimum monthly payments were the straw that broke the camel's back. I knew something was very wrong with my life. I felt disconcerted, but I didn't know what it was, let alone how to fix it. I didn't know if the feelings that I was feeling were valid or if I was just overreacting. Had I become so Americanized that I'd forgotten my cultural values?

Sitting in that parking lot, I finally acknowledged that I had been lied to in the deepest way possible. I began to wonder why I was so gullible as to buy into all the lies. What about me told him it was okay for him to treat me in this manner?

I needed and wanted so badly to understand why my life had turned out this way. It was certainly not the life I had dreamed of growing up. I saw that my life was a mess. I knew that to fix it, I would need something way bigger than me. I knew my parents couldn't fix it. I knew money wouldn't fix it. What I did know was that I needed God. Because everything else was a facade. I couldn't trust anyone. I couldn't trust myself to make good decisions. I couldn't trust my husband because he had lied to me since the beginning of our time together. He had told me lies upon lies, including what caste he belonged to.

My dad had told me that my husband belonged to the caste of untouchables. When I had asked him about it when we were still dating, he lied and said no. I would have accepted it had he said yes. I would have accepted it because he was my ticket out of my house. But he did not want to tell me for fear of losing me. From the get-go, he pretended to be someone he wasn't. As did I. I pretended to love him when I didn't. I was lying to myself, not just him. I felt so suffocated by my parents and their style of parenting that I was desperate to get out of their house. I guess he was my mirror.

Our relationship was built on the sand of lies. Neither of us was honest with the other. Apparently, we both had hidden agendas.

He pretended to be so wise that nothing perturbed him. He pretended to be so enlightened that he could accept everything. He pretended to be a saint who could forgive anything.

I thought he was kind and mature. I was desperately looking to be accepted even though I felt like "used goods," so I decided to tell him that I had been sexually abused as a child so he would know that I was not a virgin. Which was and is a big thing in the Indian culture. No one wants used goods.

I wanted him to know about the abuse for self-serving reasons. One of my biggest fears was the fear of rejection. I did not want him to find out from someone else about the sexual abuse, or for him to find out during our first sexual encounter that I was not a virgin. I was mortified at the thought of him finding out and rejecting me. I had a deep sense of shame around my sexuality. I wanted to tell him when the moment was right.

One day he had just returned from a trip to Devon Street in Chicago, Illinois. Devon Street is a one-stop destination for all things Indian, ranging from knickknacks to gold jewelry to food. If you ever walk this street, your nostrils will be inundated with a myriad of pungent smells from Indian spices available, not just the ones available for sale but the ones being cooked with. Just like the good old times when we lived on top of a bazaar in India.

I used to love panipuri from Devon Street. Panipuri is a deep-fried ball made of wheat that is stuffed with spicey water, chutney, garbanzo beans, and potatoes. When he returned from his trip to Illinois from Milwaukee, he bought some for me. We were sitting in his 1980s Toyota Camry. I watched him poke a hole in the ball with his thumb and add the water and the chaat mixture to the ball. He then proceeded to put one in my mouth. The ball burst with a rainbow of flavors in my mouth, taking me back to India.

I figured he was in a nurturing mood, so once he was done feeding me, I seized the moment and decided to tell him about the sexual abuse. It was the first time I had spoken about this to anyone.

I wanted to tell him about the abuse so there would be no surprises or secrets. I wanted him to know that I was "used goods." Apprehensively, I searched his face for a reaction. I didn't know what to expect. Was he going to reject me? Or was he going to accept me, all of me?

Finally, after a few moments of silence, he said, "Joo can have sex with somevon else right in front of me, and it vould not bother me." Relief came over me knowing he was accepting of me and my past.

You can imagine the hurt when ten years into our marriage he said to me, "I wish joo hadn't told me about the abuse. I wish joo had kept it to jorself." He said it in his thick Indian accent. He was not even a middle-school graduate. He had come to the United States as a Sikh priest when he was twenty-three years old and knew very little English. After ten years he simply could not put up with the pretense of being okay with the sexual abuse. His true feelings had begun to emerge. Or maybe they emerged sooner but I was too ignorant to notice them.

As I remained in the parking lot, my mind was reeling with all that we had been through over the last sixteen years of our marriage. All the inconsistencies. All the lies. All the betrayals. It was as if I were beginning to form new connections in my brain that were revealing all this to me.

In that moment I knew I needed help. I also knew that the only thing that could provide me the help that I needed was God. Because I needed nothing short of a miracle. But how did I go in search of God? Where did I even begin to look?

I had forsaken my roots as a child for the sake of acceptance when our family migrated to the states back in the early 1980s. I'd betrayed myself.

Then one day something began to arise from deep within me. It told me to go back to basics. It told me to go back to my roots. It said to go back to what I knew to be true about life. I thought about what this feeling of knowingness was trying to convey to me. At that moment I was so lost that I welcomed any insights and was willing to listen to the Voice of reason. Upon reflecting on it for a few minutes, I realized that what I knew to be true about life was that we are all equal and that there is one God.

In Sikhism we serve a meal at the end of every service. The meals are free. They are funded by donations to Gurdwara, the place of worship for Sikhs, and are cooked by volunteers. We all sit on the floor together to eat. This is to signify that we are all equal. No one is superior or inferior. This is because we all have the light of God within us, because we are all created equally. We all have the same blood in our veins. We all poop the same way. I had this much clarity.

Everything in America seemed topsy-turvy. Sikhism vs. Christianity, India vs. America, two completely different religions with completely different cultures, oceans apart, and little Simi stood in the middle of all the chaos that was made up of the differences between the east and the west.

In Sikhism we believe that God is within us. Christians believe Jesus to be their savior. In India we walked everywhere or used public transportation. In America people drove everywhere in their personalized tin boxes. In India we drove on the left side of the street, in America we drove on the right side. We had to push the light switch up to turn on the lights in India. In the house we lived in when we first arrived in the US, the light switch was down for on. What was a little twelve-year-old Simi to think or do? She was too busy trying to figure out what the word "is" meant. She certainly didn't have the bandwidth to study theology. She thought she didn't know anything and began to question everything.

The whirlwind in my mind that started in the early '80s was still following me as an adult. It was a twenty-six-year-long squall that was incessant. It threatened to destroy my life. Somehow, it seemed to get even stronger in this moment of financial turmoil. Not knowing what to believe, I had closed my eyes in hopes that the storm would spare me.

I had hoped that somehow things would fall into place. I was too afraid to open my eyes for fear that I would see the mess I had created. A squall threatened my existence.

This truth became my guiding light. With this principle in mind, I began my search for God within, knowing that the only thing that could get me out of the mess that I had created was this inner light that would guide my way. I began to listen to this Voice that appeared to come from somewhere deep within me. I could not point to it. But I knew to trust it, because it came through with such clarity. It came as a sense of deep knowingness; I felt the Voice internally rather than hearing an actual physical voice. When it spoke, I had no doubt. It was clear as daylight what my next steps were. I had no other choice but to begin to trust this inner Voice, as my outer world was so very confusing. The Voice became my anchor. The Voice shone light on the path that I was to walk upon. The Voice became my guide, my mentor. It had provided more clarity than the thoughts that came from my mind. It led me to read certain books and take certain classes. It brought me back to myself when I derailed. Slowly, I began to trust the Voice more and more. I knew that the Voice had my highest good in mind because I felt more at peace with the decisions it helped me to make.

When I did as the Voice said to do, I felt more at peace. The chaos in my life began to lessen. I didn't feel nearly as guilty. I had a ray of newfound hope in my heart that I had never experienced before. That's how I knew that whatever the Voice was instructing me to do was the path out of the chaos I had landed myself in ever since my family had migrated to the states.

For the first time in my life, I didn't feel helpless. For the first time in my life, I felt supported. For the first time in my life, I felt held. For the first time in my life, I felt heard. For the first time in my life, I felt nurtured. The Voice would say jump, I would say, "How high?" I began to find the way back to myself. But I knew that the journey was long and arduous. Yet I trusted this deep Voice within me to guide the way out of the darkness.

I continued to follow the Voice the best I could. One day at the end of 2011, the Voice led me to Theo. Twelve archangels forever changed the trajectory of my life. If you know anything about Sikhism, you will know that we don't believe in gods and goddesses. We don't believe in angels and archangels. But I had to trust the Voice that had guided me for almost four years. I didn't let the previous teaching from Sikhism stop me from pursuing the teaching of the archangels. I wanted to find out the truth for myself. I couldn't forsake the Voice.

The Voice was my rope that was pulling me out of the quicksand that I was in. It was my hope of being able to breathe again. So, when it told me to take classes with Theo, I jumped at the chance. I knew I could trust them to guide me. When I had a chance to speak with Theo, I said to them, "This life has been so hard," with tears streaming down my face. "We are aware," they said. "However, you are turning a corner," they went on, trying to soothe me. About a month prior to meeting Theo, I had been feeling stuck on my spiritual path, and the Voice knew that. I "stumbled" upon their website and instantly knew I had to meet them. I felt their words were written just for me. Theo promised that the inner child work would lead me to my enlightenment. That's it! That's what I had wanted! I wanted nothing more than to be enlightened. I had no idea what that meant, but I wanted it. I became eager to sign up for the classes with Theo.

During my very first class with Theo, we were all given a chance to ask Theo a question. Everyone was asking Theo about the world and where things were going. But I wanted to be selfish and ask about myself. After all, I was paying for the class, and the events of the world were the least of my concerns.

When it was my turn, I asked Theo, "What message do you have for me?"

"That point of stuck-ness that you feel will be revealed to you," they said. Boom! Way to establish trust! I had not told them that I had felt stuck on my spiritual path, but they knew it! The rest is history, as they say. I began to soak in every word that Theo would say. I didn't know how the point of stuck-ness would be revealed to me, nor did I ask. Instead, I trusted that it would be revealed to me.

Two weeks later I had a dream. A dream so vivid that it's clear as day even today, twelve years later. I hesitate to call it a nightmare, because that might imply that it was not true. When I woke up, I recalled every detail of the dream. I felt in every cell of my body that the dream was trying to tell me something. It's as if it were a deep memory stored in the cells of my body, and it had somehow arisen in the form of a dream. I had never had a nightmare before. Somewhat disoriented and intrigued by the dream, I began to write the dream down as soon as I woke up. The more I wrote, the clearer its message became. The dream was about how I was sacrificed in one of my past lives. The sacrifice was performed by my now older daughter and my husband's sister. They sacrificed me because I was "stupid." I was seven years old. After killing me, they maimed me. And I could smell some sort of meat being cooked in the pressure cooker. I felt I was reliving this whole nightmare. This explained so many things at so many different levels. It explained why my relationship was the way it was with my daughter. It explained why I felt so much animosity toward my sister-in-law at our first meeting.

At my next meeting with Theo, I asked them if what I'd witnessed in the dream was true? Was it a past life that I had encountered in my dream? Their response was a resounding, "Yes, it was," they said with a smile. Their smile was all-knowing. They paused for a moment so I could fully process the enormity of what they had just revealed to me. They knew full well how this revelation would blow open my mind to receiving the secrets of the Universe!

They knew I would begin to connect the dots. They knew it would answer all of my questions about life and rebirth. That it would clear up my thirty-year-long confusion and stop the squall. They knew this revelation would help me to understand how energy works. They knew it would help me to understand what is meant by the quote, "Energy knows no time and space." They knew the application of this knowledge would help me to solve the mysteries of physical health issues that were stemming from past lives!

Our physical body has no choice but to obey the laws of the universe. It is bound by universal principles. Until we learn what these universal laws are, we will remain bound by these laws, unable to move forward. Unable to use these laws to free ourselves. Knowledge of these laws and wisdom will help us to alleviate our suffering and lead us to our enlightenment.

I learned how a soul is recycled. I learned how a soul carries energies from different lifetimes into current lifetimes so it can heal it. Without this knowledge, the attainment of enlightenment is not possible. It was because of this past-life inner child that I had felt stuck in my path. And I could not move forward on my spiritual path until I became aware of it and began to integrate it. Their simple "yes" awakened me to the workings of the universe. The light was shining so brightly that there was no mistaking the truth. It was a moment when the bridge between heaven and earth was formed. The viaduct between science and spirituality was created. It was a moment when my soul was made privy to the innermost workings of the universe. I saw the different cog wheels of energy that were set in motion by this simple act of disclosure.

It was a moment that changed me forever. A moment that gave me permission to at least begin to trust myself. This reminded me that I have always known that the process of reincarnation was real. But I was too afraid to stand up for what I knew to be true for fear of mockery, retribution, isolation, rejection, and abandonment. Every cell of my body resonated with the vibration of this deep truth. I was never the same again.

The archangels helped me to learn to trust in myself again. To not doubt the ideas that may be shunned by others but felt true to me. They just returned my power back to me. I can still hear the multitude of musical instruments that played in my head with this revelation. All done single-handedly with a simple utterance of the word "yes."

This confirmation helped me to tie up so many loose ends. It helped me to construct the aqueduct between the east and the west. It helped me to see that Sikhism and Christianity were not so different after all. That the knowledge of reincarnation is suppressed by the churches. That Jesus's teachings are very similar to teachings of the Sikh gurus.

It helped me to realize that there are certain universal truths that transcend race, religion, creed, beliefs, cultures, and nations. That the universe is not bound by the man-made laws. It opened up my eyes to the mysteries of the universe. It helped me to see that religions divide while spirituality unites. It helped me to see that we are all made from the same fabric, fabric of a higher power that unites us all. And that higher power is called GOD.

As I began my work with Theo, I soon learned that my inner children were responsible for all of my problems that I was encountering in life. This included my financial issues, my inability to stand up for myself, my choice of husband. This also included my choice of friends and how I parented my kids. When my inner child became triggered, I traumatized my own kids, all because I was acting as a child in an adult body making adult parenting decisions.

These realizations deeply saddened me and motivated me to become a better parent. In fact, the way I treated my older daughter with anger and contempt became the impetus behind my change. This was an act of Love toward her. I did not like the person that I became when I was with her. She triggered me to no end. Even while I was pregnant with her, I had this hatred toward her. I could not figure out why, nor was I willing to admit that I felt this way. After her birth there were times when I felt so much anger toward her that I wanted to kill her. In all honesty I am surprised that I didn't. It took all I had to not kill her. Because I was supposed to feel a certain way while I was pregnant. Of course, I did not have the knowledge about past lives with her that helped to bring awareness of issues at hand.

Imagine the anger that you might feel when someone is killing you. That anger does not just simply dissipate. It remains with you until you can process it, transmute it, and clear it. How can you begin the process of healing if you are not even aware of the universal laws? We reincarnate so that we can clear these energies. Because it's only in this physical realm, the earth, that we can begin to release these pent-up energies. Hence the recycling of the soul. There is a grander purpose behind the cycle of death and rebirth.

Inner child work was the savior that I had been waiting for. When I began the work, I started to notice that I was softer when I was with my daughter. My anger toward her began to diminish. I wasn't a tyrant when I was with her. I was able to be the mother that I wanted to be to her.

As I began to do this work, I found out that each inner child had a set of beliefs that they were holding onto. These beliefs form at the moment the trauma occurs, and they run our lives. Underlying all of the beliefs is the belief of not being lovable enough, not being good enough, and not being worthy enough. This realization helped me to connect the dots for the myriad other ways my inner children were running my life. I ran away from home with a married Sikh priest who did not have my best interests in mind because my inner children neither felt safe at home nor did they feel worthy of a man who could take care of them. They felt suffocated and controlled at home, so they left without saying a word to anyone. They used adult Simi's boyfriend to leave home. The adult Simi never loved him.

Holding the belief that all men will hurt me came from my six-month-old self, who was sold for sex. Hence my difficulties in having relationships and not trusting anyone, especially men. Feeling like I was stupid and scoring a 1.8 GPA in college one semester was because of my three-year-old self, who felt so stupid that she thought studying would prove she was stupid. The big financial losses I experienced were because of my two-year-old self, who did not feel worthy.

As you can see, the inner children affect our day-to-day lives. They are the decision-makers of our life until we take charge and stop them. Ultimately, the inner children just want to be heard, seen, and loved. To be heard, seen, and loved, they will bend over backward for someone who they think might provide them with that Love and attention they are seeking. They are willing to do just about anything to be seen. They have no boundaries, and so they are pushovers and gullible.

Meeting Theo was the beginning of my learning the inner child work. At first it was difficult because this work involves getting in touch with your feelings. Because of the intense trauma we've experienced, a lot of us are numb to our feelings. We have learned to shove our feelings down. We have learned to compartmentalize them so that we can unpack them at a later time. It is now time to unpack those intense emotions. The time is right, and the time is now.

I began to practice inner child work every chance I got. It was as if my soul was thirsting for knowledge and wisdom that is contained within inner child work. With this work I began to learn to Love myself. The more I practiced this work, the deeper it took me to show me that all of my problems were stemming from the trauma I had endured as a child. Until I healed it, my problems would continue to fester. Time was not going to heal all wounds, consciousness was. And I knew that I had the power within me to heal myself. I had to take charge of my life. I knew that I was my savior. Theo taught me that no one outside of me was going to come and save me. I had to start directing which way I wanted to take life rather than letting my inner children take me somewhere I didn't want to go.

Each soul's journey is different. Not everyone is going to be ready. This could be your lifetime to rest. It is for you to self-evaluate and discern to see where you are at and if this is the right time for you to embark upon your inner journey, because as we move through this journey things can initially intensify your symptoms whether physical, mental, or emotional. For your safety and well-being, I encourage you to embark upon this journey if and when you feel that it is safe, appropriate, healthy, and timely for you to do so.

Chapter 3

The Mystical Healer

My seven-year-old self, wearing pigtails, was glued to the gray, chipped paint and rusty bars outside of my neighbor's window. From the window, I watched the hustle and bustle of the preparations for puja—a ceremony offering devotional homage and prayer to one or more deities—hosted by the neighbor lady. We were not invited because we were devout Sikhs, and this was a Hindu service. I saw people gathering around this thin lady. Everyone sat on the floor cross-legged, on the white sheets, facing this lady, who appeared to be someone important. Once seated, people surrounding her began to sing bhajans (devotional songs with religious themes). No sooner did they begin to sing than the lady's eyes started to become droopy, and her body began to rock in a circular manner. Then she began to rub both of her hands together. My eyes widened as I saw this lady manifest scarves from her hands literally from the cosmos! She then began to distribute the scarves to her devotees.

I had never seen anything like this before! How was she doing this? *Well, if she can manifest things from her hands, I can certainly heal with my hands,* I thought. Growing up in India, the paranormal was a normal way of life. It infiltrated everything we did. We heard countless stories of people being healed with simply a touch or by ingesting fruit powder that was blessed. I wanted to learn to heal in this manner. I wanted to become a great mystical healer.

The dream to become a mystical healer was shattered when my family migrated to the states. I stopped hearing stories of people who would heal mysteriously. I couldn't even talk about reincarnation without sounding weird, let alone talk about mysticism. Western medicine's grip over the Americans, combined with the church's hold on the masses, has taken the art out of healing. It has robbed people of the power to heal their physical bodies by making them dependent on pharmaceuticals and waiting for that savior to show up. It has taken the magic out of their lives. Together medicine and church have burgled people's joy from their hearts.

When, in reality, medicine and church go hand-in-hand. Done with the right intention, the marriage of medicine and church is what creates miracles. Unfortunately, both medicine and church want to control the masses instead of helping them to heal. They are both greedy and power hungry. They enjoy watching people suffer. They have intentionally created systems that have led to atrocious crimes against humanity.

For example, calcium and magnesium balance each other out in our body. Our body requires balance both outside and inside. Calcium is what we call a vasoconstrictor, meaning it constricts blood vessels. Magnesium is a vasodilator, meaning it dilates blood vessels. Owing to our agricultural practices, our soil has been depleted of magnesium. We used to get about 700 mg of magnesium per meal. Nowadays, we are lucky if we get 200 mg per meal if we eat organic. If we don't get enough magnesium, it leaves the calcium unopposed, which means the blood vessels vasoconstrict, leading to high blood pressure.

The pharmaceuticals have created a class of medications call calcium channel blockers. These medications block the calcium from binding to the receptors, which in turn leads to lowered blood pressure. Instead of giving our patients magnesium, we give them calcium channel blockers. Over the years I have given my patients magnesium and taken them off their multiple blood pressure medications. This is just one example of how we are manipulated as consumers of medicine.

It's obvious to me that since they have created a class of medications called calcium channel blockers, they know about the mechanism of action of calcium. I highly doubt they studied the mechanism of action and simply overlooked the mechanism of action for magnesium. If they did overlook the mechanism of action for magnesium, then should they be trusted with complex studies? There is study after study showing that magnesium is responsible for more than 300 different enzymatic reactions in the body, including regulation of blood pressure and diabetes. Why then is magnesium not the first line of therapy in the "evidence-based medicine guidelines"? Is the so-called evidence just being presented when it meets their agenda? Why else would they not recommend treatments they know will work? These treatments not only work, but they cure! In fact, we are taught that vitamins and minerals don't really work! If that is really the case, why is there an abundance of vitamins and minerals in natural foods? Why are the pharmaceutical companies trying to make vitamins and minerals a prescription medication? Why are we being taught lies in medical schools?

Churches also withhold information that can lead to our healing, such as the information about reincarnation as revealed by the archangels themselves. It is this knowledge that helped to put the pieces together regarding our physical bodies.

This knowledge helped me to understand how energies from past lives affect our present-day health. Suppression of this knowledge is keeping the masses from attaining their physical health. Sadly, people who speak up about it are silenced. The sleeping masses are just that…asleep, oblivious to how they are being manipulated. They blindly trust both the doctors and the priests in spite of the egregious acts being committed against them by both. I was caught in the war against humanity, with medicine and the church on either side. My dreams were crushed in this conflict, an early casualty of the ongoing hostilities.

Little Simi felt lost, confused, and cast aside. It broke my spirit to know that I could never be the mystical healer. In fact, I began to wonder if there even was such a thing. I began to doubt myself, to a point where I began to think that perhaps I was a bit crazy for wanting something different, something better for myself. As long as I questioned myself, I could not move forward in life. I could not even begin to undertake the journey toward becoming a mystical healer.

Belief is what drives us toward our goals. Belief is what drives us toward our intentions. Belief is what drives us toward our destiny. Medicine and the church in America robbed me of my destiny through the creation of self-doubt. While I admit that I allowed it and take full responsibility for it, what they have done is create the soil that breeds self-doubt through gaslighting, which then hinders the dreams and destinies of countless people. It stops us from claiming our full power as powerful divine beings. They are truly afraid to know that they will lose control if we stop doubting ourselves.

What better way to stop someone in their tracks than to have them doubt themselves? This self-doubt is poison for our dreams, our ambitions, our growth, and our transformation.

Self-doubt keeps us suppressed. It enslaves us. It stops us from reaching the summit and reaching our full potential as the image of God. Self-doubt is the killer of hope, wishes, and joy.

I know my little body, brain, and mouth felt stuck. No matter what I said, it fell on deaf ears. It was either contradicted or mocked as if I were from a different planet. Words stopped coming out of my mouth because I didn't know what to say. I slowly, over time, lost my Voice. I didn't know what to say so I stopped talking. I became quiet. Self-doubt had stolen my Voice. Our Voice is not just our spoken word. Our Voice is our higher thoughts. It is our sense of knowingness, our intuition. Our Voice is our wisdom, our inner strength, our courage. Our Voice is the impetus behind our power to stand up for ourselves. It is the impetus behind our empowered relationships. It is the power behind our financial freedom. It is our Voice that creates magic and miracles in our lives. Don't take your Voice lightly. It is YOUR power.

This is why the powers that be have tried to take your Voice away from you through creating an environment of self-doubt. I left my nine-to-five job back in 2013 because I simply didn't agree with the western medical practices to keep people dependent upon the pharmaceuticals. I don't agree with suppressing information simply for the sake of dominance over others. Since then, I have been wanting to teach people about the mind-body connection. I have tried to list my services on different freelancing sites; however, each site took down my listing, stating that it "violates their community standards." How am I violating community standards by simply offering to help people to get in touch with their bodies and their emotions? Why is that a crime? Most importantly, why am I being suppressed? Such questions beg to be discussed. Why was my Voice suppressed? I don't know about you, but I sniff tyranny.

Don't let them take freedom of choice and discovery away from you. Reclaim your Voice. Stop doubting yourself. Start to trust yourself. Trust yourself in little things so that you can trust yourself in big things. It is a daily practice. Hold hands with that inner child and give it a Voice. Allow it to speak unapologetically, uncensored.

Medicine and the church have created a society that is rigid to new ideas. Medicine has created "evidence-based medicine" as a gatekeeper to new ideas. The churches have suppressed and negated information, such as the concept of reincarnation, to serve as a gatekeeper to new ideas. By doing so they have both stopped new ideas from effecting change.

As long as people believe in these ideas that serve as the gate-keepers, growth cannot occur. It causes stagnation, and we all know that stagnation is not good for us. Stagnation in water breeds mosquitoes. Stagnation in economics breeds poverty. Stagnation in relationships breeds divorce. Stagnation in the physical body breeds illness and death. Not just physical death but the death of individualism. Death of creativity. Death of joy. Death of life.

New ideas breathe life into life. New ideas allow life to flow through us. The establishment wants to suppress new ideas because new ideas threaten their establishments. New ideas will disempower them, and they will lose hold over the masses. They will no longer be able to control the masses. So, they are trying their utmost to stop the spread of these new ideas. I can tell you that the new ideas will spread like wildfire. There is no stopping them, try as they might.

Somewhere along the way, I was sucked into taking the poison of self-doubt. I had forgotten that I wanted to become a mysti-cal healer. Self-doubt had gnawed at my dreams long enough to erode them. I thought earning a degree as a medical doctor was the best that I could do.

I felt distressed at the way we practiced medicine. The doctors all know that if you start someone on a medication for, say, high blood pressure or hypertension (HTN), that it was only a matter of time before you started them on an endless round of different medications. On average, a person with HTN is on three to four different medications. Clearly, the suppression of HTN with medications was leading to the need for as many as four different medications. How come no one saw that? Why isn't anyone speaking up? Oh, wait, that's because we are practicing "evidence-based medicine." So that makes it okay. It is a permission to keep adding medications even when you know they are not going to work or may even be making an illness worse through suppression of symptoms. The perks of practicing "evidence-based medicine" is that no one can sue you. No one can touch you with a ten-foot pole. No one can come after you. Your license and livelihood are safe even if you screw up someone else's livelihood.

But even if you wanted to talk to someone about it, who would you talk to? What would you say without being discredited? Where do you even begin a conversation such as this? Who is going to listen? Everyone just shoves it under the rug and goes about their daily business. We are too busy to fight this injustice. Ignorance is bliss, I suppose, until it isn't. I was given a bad evaluation by a cardiologist when I questioned the use of aspirin. I wasn't saying he was wrong or that he shouldn't use it, but I was simply asking questions. Apparently, that threatened his sense of self enough that he wanted to shut down my questioning. Do we not learn by asking questions? Isn't that what critical thinking is all about? Shouldn't questioning be encouraged if we are dealing with someone's life? I hope you want me to question things if you are ever on a hospital bed fighting for your life. I hope that someone else asks questions on my behalf as well.

Luckily for me, by then I had started listening to the Voice. But the listening didn't happen until I was drowning in my life. It took that kind of intensity for me to go past the self-doubt and begin to listen to the Voice that was arising from within me. Seeing my life in shambles, I knew something had to give. I needed to start somewhere, and that somewhere was within. Because everything outside of me had failed me. That's when I went in search of a teacher who would teach me the art of looking within. That too was inspired and guided by the Voice.

During the classes, Theo had also reminded me of my desire to be that mystical healer. Not only did they remind me but encouraged me to follow through with my dream. They went on to say that "it is quite admirable" that I wanted to become that kind of a healer. From that moment on, my desire to become the mystical healer was rekindled. Theo's words broke through the wall of all the self-doubt I had built. I never looked back.

I cannot even begin to describe or put into words what the inner child work has done for me. It has given me a second chance at life. It gave me the courage to release self-doubt and to trust myself again. It gave a renewed sense of hope. It gave me a glimpse into my future. It empowered me to take charge of my life and to guide my life-ship in the trajectory that I wanted to go in. I became the helmsman of my lifeboat. I began to live my life on my terms. I began to decide which lessons I wanted to learn. I began to align my free will with the divine will so I could navigate through the treacherous waters I had landed myself in through my karmic actions. I began to trust myself to know that I needed to hand my life over to God if I am to extricate myself from the mess that I had created.

It all began with me ending my marriage of twenty years. It was one of the hardest things I have ever done. Theo had encouraged me to get a divorce, but not in so many words. They hinted that I think I can change my husband, but I can't. That I am in an abusive relationship. They also said that if I choose to let go of my marriage, then I will find my peer. That I am not meant to be alone. I was shocked that the archangels would even imply that I get a divorce. Because aren't we supposed to stay together "until death do you part," as they say? I was still doubting their message when I was sitting in meditation two weeks later, and I heard that I needed to let my relationship go. That was the final straw in deciding that I was ready for a divorce.

I had to trust that the guidance that I was receiving was correct. That it was coming from a divine source and not my ego. I can't say that it has always been easy for me to trust myself and the guidance that I am receiving. I do know that it is important for me to trust enough to follow the guidance with action steps. I had been thinking about divorcing my husband for the last ten years of my twenty-year-long marriage. In fact, I thought about it every day, several times a day. But I didn't have the courage to follow through with it until I started doing the inner child work.

What this situation taught me was that if you think about something that much, you should probably go do it (and I don't mean self-harm). I know now that it was the Voice talking that was telling me to go get a divorce. But for fear of being alone, I could not hear it. Frankly, until I followed this guidance I could not move forward toward my destiny, and the Voice knew that. Hence its persistence to get me to file for a divorce. Because the Voice knew that without first taking this step, I was stuck.

A few days after finalizing my decision and asking my husband for a divorce, my gifts began to open up. I began to experience what it would be like to step into my power as a healer. I was finishing up another spiritual class while taking classes with Theo. In my other class I came across a fellow student. Harald is from Germany and was seventy years old at the time. We connected via Facebook and email. He had asked for prayers in the Facebook group as he was about to undergo surgery for an abdominal hernia. A month later he requested another set of prayers because he had developed an abscess at the site of the surgery. Another month later he was asking for more prayers because he had now developed a hematoma. Lo and behold, he was back again asking for prayers another month later. He was afraid that he might not wake up from general anesthesia, as he was about to go for his fourth surgery, for a wound that had turned into a seroma. Any medical practitioner can tell you that, on average, seromas take three to four months to heal, and they (more than likely) will leave a disfiguring scar. Which means that there will be another surgery whether or not the seroma heals.

He shared with me via email that he had been married to his wife for fifty years but had been estranged from her for the last twenty years even though they lived in the same house as roommates. When I read this, I received my very first download ever. I had never had a download before. I received a group of thoughts that gave me the solution to his problems. I don't know where they came from, but it made sense. I knew these were not my thoughts because I did not have the capacity to think like that. It was clear as a bell. It came through with such purity that I felt compelled to listen to it. The download said that this gentleman needed to heal his relationship with his wife for the wound to heal.

Yet, I questioned, "Is this really what needs to happen for the wound to heal?" The Voice told me to trust the message. Trust what I was receiving. That I received this message because I had trusted in the process when I asked my husband for a divorce. In that faith-based action I had opened up the space to receive messages such as this. I knew if I didn't follow through, I would never know whether the message was correct or not, and I would end up back on square one and that was getting stuck again. I did not want to get stuck again. After all, I'd only thought about the divorce for ten years before acting on it. I couldn't risk it again. I had to trust that what I was receiving was appropriate. I couldn't let that hard work go in vain because it had taken a lot of courage for me to begin the process of trusting. I had worked hard at opening myself up to receiving the guidance, I certainly couldn't stop now. I gathered the nerve and wrote the email to my newfound acquaintance.

I wrote an email and shared the message that I had received with him. At first, he became quite defensive and told me to leave his wife out of this. That his wife was not a part of this spiritual class. Again, I had to push through my fear of being wrong and go past my self-doubt. I listened very closely to hear how the Voice wanted me to respond. The Voice told me to stand my ground and to not let fear deter me from what I knew and felt to be the truth. I wrote the email exactly as the Voice guided me to. I responded by telling him not to shoot the messenger. Not only that, but this also sounded like a lesson that he needed to learn. I also told him that the choice was his as to whether or not he wanted to follow through with the guidance that was coming forth. But he needed to know that if he didn't learn his lesson at this time, it would definitely present itself again at a later time, and perhaps even in a future lifetime. The lessons don't go away just because you change bodies. This situation is here to help him to heal a deeper issue. He could rise to the occasion or ignore it. It was his choice.

With that said, I hit the send button. A part of me knew that he was going to rise to the occasion because the Voice knew exactly what to say to get him to think and act in a manner that was in his highest good.

He waited a couple of days before responding. He told me that he had contemplated what I wrote in the email and had decided to take "baby steps." He told me he was going to give his wife unconditional Love. After all, that was the lesson we were learning in our spiritual class that we were taking together. I told him that was a great baby step and encouraged him to follow through. The Voice told me to not tell him that it was not a baby step.

A couple of weeks went by, and I didn't hear anything from him. I wrote him another email asking how things were going. He wrote back to me, saying that not only did he rekindle his relationship with his wife within two days, but his wound healed completely after ten days without leaving a disfiguring scar. There was no need for a fourth surgery. He was enjoying his rekindled relationship with his wife. He thanked me for my help and that was the last time I heard from him.

I was honored to partake in Harald's healing. I had only heard about such miracles, but now I had helped to create one. This was truly a dream come true. This validated my concerns about the dishonest practices of our medical system. This helped me to see how self-doubt had held me in a squall for so long. This helped me to see the importance of trust in oneself. This also confirmed that my desire is my intuition. My desire to be a mystical healer was my intuition guiding me. When we doubt ourselves, we lose touch with our desires. We become numb to what it is that we really want in life.

Of course, I began to question everything I had been taught in medical school. I questioned our so-called evidence-based medicine. There is no research that could have guided Harald's healing. No amount of evidence, no number of pharmaceuticals, no amount of blood work, and no amount of imaging could have helped with the healing.

The Voice taught me to use the information learned in medical school and integrate it with what I was learning. That's when I realized that medical school gave me the scientific background of an illness. Releasing self-doubt gave me the knowledge and wisdom about the root cause of a disease. Emotions are at the root of any physical illness. It is that simple, and there are no exceptions.

I began to apply this way of practicing medicine in an urgent care setting. Of course, I was quiet about it because I did not want to be reported to the administration, so I was very discerning as to who I worked with.

It was my day to work an urgent care shift. There was a six-foot-tall patient with blond hair and blue eyes, who presented with symptoms of claustrophobia. Luckily, we were not busy that day. When I went in to evaluate him, he told me to leave the door open. I did as he wished.

Upon obtaining history he shared with me that he was a hunter and that he tracked his prey. The Voice told me the reason he was so afraid was because he picked up on the fear of the animals he was tracking. The Voice also told me that we don't pick up emotions that are not within us. The only way for someone else's emotion to stick to us is if we carry that emotion in our energy field.

Knowing this information, I asked him if he was open to something different that I had to offer, and he said yes. I was able to help him to tune into the inner child who was carrying a similar fear. Once he was aware of this fear, he was able to release it. To dissolve an emotion or a feeling, all that is needed is simply our presence. All that is required is our conscious attention to the emotion. The key is to become aware of the emotion that is related to the physical illness. As you begin to tune in, you will notice that each emotion has a slightly different vibration. Tuning into this vibration is important. With energy work the more specific you can get, the greater the healing. After about forty-five minutes of my guiding him on how to tune into his emotions, he was able to dissolve the emotion, leading him to be free of his fear of closed spaces.

Once he felt better, he leaned back in his chair and pointed to the door and said, "You can close the door now." I got up to close the door, then returned to my stool. As soon as I sat down, he leaned forward toward my five foot, one inch frame with his tall frame, looked at me intently with his blue eyes, and said, "I don't know what the fuck you did…but it worked!" His intense face turned into a smile. He had me terrified for a moment, thinking I had done something wrong. Self-doubt will creep up any chance it gets. It is up to us to continue to remain anchored in our conviction.

The more I practiced medicine in this way, the more I saw how useless the blood work, the imaging, the surgeries, and the pharmaceuticals are. I began to see even more clearly how the medications were masking the symptoms while the disease progressed, giving a misleading sense of wellness. Not only that, but the medications are also further compressing the energies, making it difficult to have an emotional release. It is my sense that medications block the emotional body from releasing emotions. This is why an illness presents with more of a vengeance—because the emotions need an outlet. The more you try to compress these energies, the more they will push back and the more they will come out with intensity. This is implied in a quote by Hippocrates, who was known as the father of western medicine, when he said, "It is not so important to know what kind of a disease a person has, but rather to know what kind of a person has the disease." Yet this foundational principle is not taught anywhere in medical schools. Such deceitful acts are inexcusable.

Imagine integrating your inner child to heal yourself from any disease ranging anywhere from high blood pressure to cancer to an open wound, without the side effects of expensive medications, radiation exposing imaging, or the cost of doctor's visits. It is free, effective, and permanent. But nothing in life comes without a price.

Inner child work can be challenging, and there is a learning curve associated with it. Just as your biological children go through different stages of development, so do your inner children. And it can be tricky to keep up with all of their developmental stages. This can be a daunting task, as your inner child will go through all of the developmental stages that you, as an adult, have to help them navigate through. This also means you will need to become aware of these various stages as your inner child goes through them. This can become intimidating as we are multidimensional beings. Every inner child has different dimensions to them. You will have to tend to their emotional well-being, their desire to be a part of a family so they can have a sense of belonging; their desire to be social; their desire to be sexual. It will become important for you, the adult, to discern where your feelings are stemming from so you can gauge whether you want to participate in a certain activity. This means that you will need to become aware of the inner child and what their needs are at any given moment. As multidimensional beings, we have to address all of the aspects of our inner children. As the emotions of your inner child surface, they can cause new illness or intensify the symptoms of an old one. You will have to pay close attention to this.

For this reason, as your inner child goes through different phases of development, you will both need support. You will require Love and understanding for the inner child and knowledge, wisdom, and compassion for the adult you so that you can learn to navigate your inner world. It is my intention to build in this support for both you and your inner child, giving both of you a safe space to heal, integrate, and begin to trust again.

An understanding of the metaphysical aspect of the physical body is necessary if we are to take charge of our health. We have a physical body, which is layered with an etheric body followed by an emotional body followed by a mental body and so on and so forth. There are many other bodies beyond the mental body. But for our purposes we just need to know about these four bodies.

According to research done by Dr. Alberto Villoldo, at the time you experience trauma the memories of the trauma get imprinted in your energy field electronically, and you can't help but to think the same thoughts repeatedly. This is because memories have an electrical charge to them, and each memory has a vibration that is electric. An illness begins with a negative thought. Negative thoughts are produced by trauma that we endure. The negative thoughts trickle down to the emotional body, causing certain feelings. These feelings then get translated into hormones in the physical body.

Each body has a language of its own. The mental body's language is thoughts and images. The emotional body's language is feelings and emotions. These feelings and emotions cause a pitting in the etheric body, which sends the signal to the physical body to produce certain hormones. The hormones and biochemical changes are the language of the physical body.

For instance, if you keep thinking, "There's a tiger, there's a tiger, there's a tiger," this thought will lead you to feel anxious, whether or not there is a tiger. An anxious feeling leads to the production of the hormone cortisol, among others. Chronic cortisol secretion, over time, causes weight gain, type 2 diabetes, heart disease, autoimmune diseases, cancer, and a multitude of other illnesses, if not all of them. A negative thought is the root cause of a disease. There are many who use this example, yet few know how to work through it.

Let's look at a working definition of the mind. The mind is not the brain. The mind is an abstract concept. We all have one mind. The mind was created by God to simply function as a vessel to transport information from a higher source into the brain. That no longer remains the case when the mind is split because of trauma. When you experience trauma, the mind splits into a higher and a lower mind. The lower mind is what we commonly refer to as the ego. It's the constant mind chatter that you may experience. It's the trauma that causes the formation of the ego. The ego is born out of our need for protection from traumatic events we may incur.

Trauma is anything that you perceive to be traumatic. It doesn't matter if it is something little or something big. They both equally affect your mind. Anytime you experience trauma you form a set of beliefs that help you to get through life while trauma is occurring. This is your psyche's way of protecting you. You can see this reflected in my six-year-old inner child, who was sexually abused because her mother left her in the care of people who were untrustworthy. My six-year-old self formed the belief that she is not important enough. If she were important enough, then her mother would pay attention to her. I formed the belief so I wouldn't keep hoping that my mother would come and save me from the abuse. It was too painful to think that she didn't want to save me. I now know that my mom is a narcissist and felt too overwhelmed with the responsibility of taking care of a child. It was less painful to think that I just wasn't important to her. The emotional pain of being rejected by my mother was far greater than the belief that I must not be important enough.

The beliefs we form when a trauma occurs stay with us for as long as we live and carry over to our adult relationships when we get older. Because this universe is magical and we are the creators of our own reality, we manifest what we believe. As an adult, if you have the belief that you are not important enough, then your mind will create situations to reflect that belief over and over. We can begin to shift our reality when we make a conscious effort to shift these limiting beliefs. These limiting beliefs are held in place by the inner child. These beliefs will remain in place and will continue to navigate your life until you integrate the fragmented part of you, because when you integrate the fragmented part, it no longer feels unsafe. When the fragment feels safe it will release those limiting beliefs, because it no longer needs those beliefs for the sake of survival.

If the trauma accumulates, it causes irreversible damage to the psyche. Each time we incarnate, we bring forward the trauma from previous lifetimes. If we didn't, how else can we heal it?

Death does not release us from ourselves. It does not change us, our habits, or our patterns. We remain as we are until we do our inner work. Until we integrate the fragmented parts of ourselves.

The intensely dark childhood trauma caused a severe split in my mind so that I developed eighteen multiple personalities. There was one who was subservient to her husband; then there was one who was a tyrant to her daughter. There was one who felt helpless, while there was one who emerged as grandiose, and the list went on. Together these personalities formed a persona that we call narcissism.

I presented myself as humble on the outside, yet felt like I was better than others on the inside. That I was the most special person in the world. It was my little secret. What I didn't know was that what I thought was a secret was not such a big secret, because I hardly made any friends. Looking back, I realize that the people who were not traumatized saw right through me and walked away from me. And the people who were traumatized were only skilled at having dysfunctional relationships and would cause more hurt. I was not capable of having intimate relationships either. The split in my mind was so deep that the desire to love someone was just as strong as the desire to hurt that same person. The desire to be with someone was just as strong as the desire to run away from them. I was blind to who I had become and couldn't figure out why I didn't have a great relationship with my daughters, why I couldn't find an intimate partner, why I didn't have close friends, why I was alone all the time, why I didn't get invited to parties and weddings or even an afternoon coffee, why I never had an occasion to dress up. I missed out on all the fun little moments of life. Living an isolated life is heartbreaking and maddening. The saddest thing was that I was stuck in my sick mind like a prisoner, and I couldn't run away from myself. No matter where I went, there I was. To say that this has been a painful life would be an understatement. I had no choice but to befriend my inner children. Sitting in the prison of my mind, I had no choice but to go into the darkness of my mind to look for a way to extricate myself out of my misery. No one could have done this work for me; I became my own savior.

The Voice told me that the damage to the psyche is irreversible and presents itself as narcissism and is the foundation for all other mental illnesses. The root of narcissism is deeply etched in shame, self-doubt, and inferiority. I felt extremely insecure about who I was and carried so much of my shame around my unworthiness that I created a separate persona around me. To make up for the deep sense of unworthiness, I pretended to myself that I was better than anyone else. I pretended that I was more special than anyone else in this world. I pretended that I was more powerful than anyone else in this world. This, of course, came across as grandiosity. In fact, I often wondered why other people didn't see my importance and specialness. I pretended long enough that I believed in it. This mindset offered safety to my different personalities.

Yet my outward appearance reflected my innermost secret that even I was not aware of. I appeared to be meek and timid, almost mousy. The fear I felt on the inside had created an outward persona that was very visible in my physical appearance. I abhorred how I looked. I wanted to look empowered and powerful but didn't know what I could do to shift my looks so I didn't appear slow or challenged. My self-talk was filled with vengeance because of my appearance. And somehow, I thought that the negative self-talk would miraculously make me look different, that somehow my body would cooperate and give me the curves exactly where I wanted them.

This false persona of self created a shell around me. A bubble of sorts. A shell that no one was allowed to penetrate. I was afraid that if someone penetrated the shell, they would find out who I really was. I didn't allow people to get too close to me. Just the thought of someone finding out who I really was underneath the persona melted me into a pile of shame. Yet I craved intimacy and deeper connection and was oblivious as to why I couldn't have them. It was duality at its best.

The shame I felt was deep and had a stronghold on me. I wanted to keep this facade at all costs, because underneath the facade was a very insecure and fragile child who was sitting in the darkness of shame. The pain and the shame of unworthiness was so deep that I became emotionally unavailable and cold. It made me appear like I lacked empathy, when in reality I was already in so much emotional pain that I couldn't bear to feel the pain of another. I felt so ashamed that I was drowning in my own pain. How could I let anyone into my world? I was happy being an introvert. I felt awkward and could feel myself acting weird and feeling uncomfortable in social situations. Oftentimes I didn't know what to say. I didn't know what to ask the other person to carry on a conversation. I would find myself getting lost in my own thoughts while someone was talking. But smiling and agreeing allowed the other person to not see that I had checked out.

Years of inner child work prepared me to see the persona that I had built around me. It helped to strengthen my core through releasing shame, self-doubt, and feelings of inadequacy so that I could see what I was doing and who I had become as a result. So I could see the monster that I had become. So I could see the pain that I was causing others. Once I saw the persona, I was able to accept it. By virtue of acceptance, the persona dissolved. While it was a painful process to look at the persona

I had created and how I was hurting myself and others, it was just as rewarding when it dissolved. This realization helped me to see why my life was the way it was, why I had no friends, why I had no partner. How this was affecting my financial health. How this was affecting my physical health. This kind of self-awareness and self-actualization was not possible without inner child work.

As long as I carried the false persona, I could not become the mystical healer that I had wanted to become and shine my light in its fullness. I needed to heal the shame, the self-doubt, and the feeling of unworthiness so I could realize my divinity. How could I shine my light brightly when I thought lowly of myself, when I berated myself, when I abhorred myself, when I was ashamed of myself? To do this work is a great act of self-Love. If you don't do it, no one else can do it for you. It is your journey and yours alone. If you don't do it now, you will have to do it at some point along the way. There is no moment like the present moment to start your excursion. This is the greatest gift you will ever give yourself. Let the voyage begin, and don't stop.

Chapter 4

Russian Dolls

Maybe you are searching among branches,
for what only appears in the roots.

—Rumi

I LEFT OFFICE HOURS BEHIND WITH my job as an urgent care provider in September of 2013. I left because I saw the way that we practiced medicine is not really medicine. It is trickery. Medicine is one of the few professions when you graduate you start making at least six figures right off the bat. I became a rubber stamp for the pharmaceutical industry the moment I graduated. I was used as a pawn. I was "encouraged" to follow the "evidence-based guidelines." And if I didn't, I would get reprimanded by the administration, by the insurance companies, and even get dirty looks from other providers. Under the guise of evidence-based medicine, I could make all the mistakes I wanted. The patient wouldn't be able to touch me in a court of law as long as I followed the evidence-based guidelines.

No matter how you slice or dice it, evidence-based medicine is simply a Band-Aid that will necessitate more Band-Aids down the road. No matter how many double-blind, randomized, placebo-controlled studies you run, you are still searching for a Band-Aid. No matter how large the study is, it is not your body they are studying. It may be a representation of your body, but it is not your body. It is simply a way to keep you searching outside of you for what is inside of you.

Your body has a body composition that is unique to you. Your body knows about the genetic trauma that is passed on from your ancestors that is affecting your DNA. Why do you think certain diseases are said to be carried in your DNA? It's because trauma affects your DNA by mutating it. The mutation is then passed on to you in the form of an illness. Genetic illness is nothing but a mutation in your DNA caused by trauma to your ancestors. Your ancestors were not able to heal the trauma, so it was passed onto you. It is not a death sentence. You have the power within you to create alchemy, to shift energy, to heal your DNA.

No study can ever tell you what your body needs. No study can ever tell you what your body wants so it can heal itself by itself. You can wait for the latest study to tell you which drug to take for heart disease or diabetes or cancer, but these medications suppress your symptoms at best. At worst they will kill you, because the disease continues to progress with these medications, while the symptoms are suppressed. It's no different than, say, when you have a broken leg due to an injury and you take Vicodin. While Vicodin may alleviate the pain temporarily, it cannot heal the injury. Just because the pain has lessened or even been temporarily alleviated, that doesn't mean you should walk on your broken leg. Because if you do, it will cause further injury. An illness is the same way. In fact, when you suppress an illness with medication, the illness will resurface in another lifetime. There is no escaping an illness. In this case, in death you do not part.

Usually when a disease presents itself, it is trying to tell you something. It is telling you that you have an emotion(s) that is blocking the flow of your energy causing a state of disease or feeling uncomfortable. It is just trying to tell you that your energy is stuck. That's it! It's that simple. If you don't deal with it, the energy will remain stuck until the time you untangle it so it can begin to flow again. It will continue to get layered and compressed until you are ready to deal with it. The longer you wait, the longer it will take you to get it to flow again. So, you might as well start now.

Don't wait for that next study to give you permission to go within. The medical establishment will never give you that permission because they have too much to lose. They have invented systems to keep you stuck and suffering. Medical insurance was partly invented so you would run to the doctor every time you got sick instead of looking within to see where the block is. You have given your power away to doctors who know nothing about you. They may know something about the human body, but they know nothing about *your* body. There is a big difference!

They know nothing about the things that influence your health. Such as your conditioning from your past lives, the Karma you have created, or your ancestral trauma that is causing a mutation in your DNA. Nor can they ever know. The beauty of this work is that you don't have to know either. You simply have to tune into your inner child and integrate that part of you for healing to happen. Because the effects of integration ripple through different dimensions and heal your past and future lives for a complete and permanent healing. This is how powerful you are!

One day, while I was still working as an urgent care provider, I was approached by my physician's assistant (PA), whom I will call Amy. She was about twelve weeks pregnant at the time. She told me that she was having some vaginal bleeding and was wondering if I could check her out. I agreed to work her up. After I obtained a history, did the physical exam, and ordered blood work, I sent her over for an ultrasound. While she was getting the ultrasound, I was approached by my medical assistant (MA). My MA said, "Did you know that Amy was upset because she could not get her insurance to cover the ultrasound so she could see the sex of the baby?" I said, "No," because I had not known. But as soon as my MA said that it all made sense.

Amy had wanted an ultrasound but did not want to pay for it. So, her mind created a situation in which the insurance company paid for the ultrasound, and Amy didn't have to pay for it. Her ultrasound results came back normal, and she carried the pregnancy to term without any further complications. She delivered a healthy baby at term.

I share this story to elicit the power of the mind to create an illness based on our hidden agendas. She could not fight with the insurance company to get them to cover the ultrasound. But she created a situation in which the insurance company had to cover the ultrasound as a part of the evaluation for vaginal bleeding. Obtaining an ultrasound for vaginal bleeding during pregnancy is in the evidence-based guidelines. In this case, the evidence-based guidelines backfired. I am sure this was not the first time, nor will it be the last time.

Energy is powerful. It can kill just as it can heal. It's what you do with it. As you do your inner child work, you will learn the art of working with energy so that you can create alchemy. We are all alchemists. We have just forgotten who we are. When you embark on the inner child train you will begin to remember how to create alchemy pretty quickly because the 5D (fifth dimension) energies that are on our earth right now are supporting our remembrance. They are supporting us stepping into our divinity. Creating alchemy is our birthright.

I was nine years old at the time. It was a hot summer evening. We had a net set up for badminton in our large balcony that served as a canopy to the shop beneath us. I was playing badminton with my cousins, who had been molesting me since I was six years of age. One of my cousins served the birdie, and I hit the birdie diagonally and it landed on the ground in front of the shop underneath us. I did this repeatedly. Every time it was my turn to hit the birdie, it landed downstairs. I didn't know why I couldn't hit it straight. This was not the first time I had played badminton. Frustrated, my cousins stopped me from playing. They told me to leave. I went inside the house and felt so irate that I began to throw the sheets and pillows on the dusty cement floor. Then I went into the kitchen to grab the steel plates and glasses and began to throw those on the floor as well. I felt enraged and wanted to express it.

When my mom returned home, she came to a house that looked like it had been hit by a hurricane. When she saw the mess I had made, she went batshit crazy on me. She never asked me about what happened or why I did what I did. She just started to hit me. At first with her hands. There was no area of my body that was off limits. Then she took off her shoe and began to hit me with her shoe. Luckily, she didn't wear heels. Afterward, she felt so guilty that she took me to the bazaar and bought me some nail polish. I guess that was her way of apologizing. In her defense, even if she had asked me why I did what did, I could not have told her.

As an adult, when I began my integration process with this nine-year-old inner child, I developed a rash on my left leg. I had never had this rash before. It was itchy and blistery and it looked angry. It appeared that it might leave a scar when it healed. Knowing what I knew, I tuned in, and I saw that my nine-year-old self was still seething at how she was treated unfairly by her mother, and that she was scratching the inside of my leg with her nails to get my attention. This in turn was causing the rash on my leg. Even though the insult was energetic I had a physical rash. It took nearly three months to soothe this little part of me. The moment I soothed her is the moment the rash went away, never to appear again and leaving without a scar.

This incident shows how trauma affects us energetically and how energy affects us physically. Our thoughts are energy. Simply by thinking the thought of scratching my leg from the inside created a rash on the outside. All matter is energy. This is truly not rocket science. Energy is what we are. The sooner you can learn to apply this concept to your health, the quicker you will heal. Einstein told us that we are all energy more than a century ago. What are we waiting for? Another study to tell us that we are energy?

Since I witnessed Harald's healing, which happened with the help of my very first download, I never looked at medicine the same way again. The Voice told me to think of everything in terms of energy. This universe is made up of energy. Vitamin B12 is energy. Magnesium is energy. Blood is energy, the liver is energy. *Everything* is energy. The only difference is the vibration. It's the vibration that makes things appear different when they are not. The only difference between a boulder and a human body is the vibration of energy. Human energy vibrates at a much higher frequency than a boulder. Imagine a Ferris wheel turning, the force that makes it turn is what we call energy. If you put a stopper that stops the Ferris wheel from turning, the stopper is a different kind of energy. It's a denser energy or a lower frequency of energy. Our body works the same way. We remain healthy as long as there is no obstruction to the flow of energy. Negative emotions slow down the flow of energy, causing an illness. When you release the negative emotion the energy in your body begins to flow again, unobstructed, giving you your health back.

To give you a better understanding of energy that is of high vibrational frequency versus energy that is low vibrational frequency, imagine when you feel good about yourself or you feel good about the circumstances of your life. That feeling is a high vibrational frequency of energy. Now imagine when you are feeling down, depressed, anxious, or worried. These feelings are of lower vibrational frequency.

Now think of an illness in terms of vibration. When we are healthy, our energy is flowing, and we vibrate at a high frequency. When we are sick, it's because something is either slowing down the flow of energy or blocking the flow of energy. The only thing that can slow down or block a high vibrating object is a low vibrating object. Imagine if you are traveling at high speed on the highway and all of a sudden, a boulder is dropped in front of you. It will stop you dead in your tracks if it doesn't kill you. Our bodies are no different.

Our body simply responds to the high and low vibrations that it encounters. These vibrations enter our body by the way of thoughts. Thoughts that create higher emotions such as joy, peace, and abundance keep our energy flowing smoothly, which in turn keeps us healthy because these emotions are of higher vibration. When you are thinking thoughts that produce these emotions, your cells respond to them by vibrating at a high frequency. Think of your cells as trillions of tiny cars traveling at a very high speed. Now imagine that you experience trauma, and suddenly you start to think thoughts that produce anger and blame. The energy of anger and blame is of a lower vibration and will slow down your cells. Now your cells will vibrate much more slowly if they don't stop. This lower vibration manifests as an illness in your body.

That's exactly what happened to Harald. He was able to choose thoughts of Love instead of anger. My guess is that it was his inner child who was holding onto the anger just like the nine-year-old in me was. By choosing Love, Harald was able to dissolve the anger. The moment he chose Love is the moment his cells began to vibrate with a higher frequency. Anger was like a boulder he was holding onto. The boulder was stopping the energy from flowing and was going to kill him had he not chosen Love. His non-healing surgical wound was telling him that there was a boulder preventing him from healing. Once he removed the boulder, the cells were able to perform their function to heal the body. Do you think another surgery would have helped him release his anger?

Now, I realize that making such a choice does not come easy, because we as humans tend to hold onto things until something tells us otherwise. In Harald's case, he had been angry with his wife for the past twenty years. It wasn't until his life was at stake that he was willing to choose Love. So, the disease presented itself to help him see what he was doing to his body by holding onto anger. His motivation to heal had to exceed his desire to hold onto spite for his wife. That moment couldn't come until he said *enough*. Until he said, "I am no longer willing to hold onto this anger because I want to heal more than I want to punish my wife."

Ultimately, all that was required was his little bit of willingness to choose Love. But that willingness didn't come easy. He had not been able to choose Love in the past. Did he want to remain angry, or did he want to get well? It was simply a matter of choice. But it only happened when his desire to heal exceeded his desire to hate. For that shift to happen, he had to suffer. In his suffering, he realized what was more important to him—his health or his anger. As Ram Dass once said, "Suffering is grace."

The more I contemplated Harald's case, the more I realized that it is simply applying Einstein's concept that we are all energy. I began to wonder why we don't apply this principle in the practice of medicine. Given all the technological advancements in our world, the current practice of medicine seems a bit archaic to me. We are still cutting people open when all we have to do is simply turn within and release the emotion that is blocking the flow of energy. I can totally see what Einstein was saying. Now, don't get me wrong. E does not equal MC-squared in my head. But I do know that we are all energy. And if we are all energy, we can shift the energy to a desirable vibration at any time. All we need is to learn how to do it. Inner child work is the tool that will help you to shift energy. It may take some time to learn how to shift the energy, but we have the power within us to shift it. That is what is called alchemy. Creating alchemy is one of our superpowers.

According to the first Law of Thermodynamics, energy cannot be created nor destroyed. It can certainly be transformed, as in Harald's case, as in the hunter's case, and in the cases of countless others that I have helped in my small private practice. This is not woo-woo stuff, but quantum physics, and it works like a charm every time! "All that is required is a little bit of your willingness"—Helen Schucman, *A Course in Miracles*.

When was the last time you went to a doctor's office and he told you to shift your energy to heal your illness? He likely isn't even aware of the concept. So how can he begin to teach his patients when he has not learned the art of energy healing himself? When he is brainwashed by the concept of evidence-based medicine, he cannot think outside the box of evidence-based medicine.

The box of evidence-based medicine serves its purpose. It keeps people from looking into holistic approaches to medicine, which, if taken seriously, could threaten the billion-dollar industry that is western medicine. It keeps one trapped outside themselves, looking outside for answers when they should be looking inward. This industry keeps hundreds of millions of patients chasing their tails for years, often their entire lifetimes. The system is rigged. But the healing you search for lies within, as you are the mystical healer.

We are alchemists at our very core. We have the power to turn disease into ease. To create alchemy, we simply need to shift our perspective. The way to shift our perspective is to feel the emotion that the inner child is feeling, fully, to be fully present to the feelings that this inner child is feeling, whether it's a feeling of betrayal, resentment, or shame. When we have felt all the feelings to their fullest extent, we come to a place of acceptance. That is what we call forgiveness. When a particular act of harm toward us ceases to elicit a negative emotion within us, we will know that we have forgiven. Forgiveness leads to our healing.

I started working on forgiving my mom when I met Theo in the beginning of 2012. When I found the inner child who was angry with her, I began my work on feeling my anger and releasing it. Since starting my work with Theo, I had written countless forgiveness letters, but still, like a hungry bulldog with a bone that I couldn't chew, I would not allow myself to completely let go of my anger even after eleven years of this work. I was stuck in that energy. I knew that the anger was affecting my life in many different ways: my finances, relationships, even my physical health. Yet I was adamant about holding onto it.

Toward the end of this chapter of my journey, the Voice guided me to take magic mushrooms. It knew I was having a difficult time forgiving my mother. It also knew it was essential for me to forgive her, as forgiveness would be the next step forward on not just my spiritual path but a step toward living the kind of life I wanted to live. Knowing these truths in my heart did not stop me from holding onto that anger for dear life. I knew I needed help if I wanted to move forward.

To continue my journey, I began to microdose on psilocybin. One particular day, I was guided by the Voice to take more than usual. That was the day that I went on a journey to a past life with my mom. I must've been ready to see that part of the relationship. It was the 800s, and in this lifetime we were both married to a king, who is my father in this current lifetime. To my shock and surprise, the king had a harem of forty wives; I was wife number one, and my mother was wife number four. I kept all the other wives in their place and made sure that my king was happy. But I noticed that the king was taking more of a liking to his wife number four, which sparked jealousy in me.

One night, when she was alone, I went quietly into her room. She was sitting in a chair in front of a mirror getting ready for the king for the night. I approached her from behind while pulling out my knife, and in one quick motion I thrust her head back by her hair and slit her throat. It was that quick and easy for me. I then left her room and simply closed the door behind me, telling the guards to take care of her. I had no remorse about it. It was a cold-blooded murder. I did not spare a second thought to it, as this was not my first murder in that lifetime—I had personally taken the lives of ten other women and ordered the deaths of many more.

When I realized what I had done to my mother, my deep rage quickly transformed into sincere apologies. I could finally see why my mother treated me the way she did. This experience on psilocybin made clear to me why our relationship was always so troubled. It explained why there was so much animosity between us. It showed me why I wasn't close to my mom. I saw why my mother had been jealous of me growing up. I also saw why she is the way she is. I saw where her narcissism stems from. I stopped blaming her and took on the responsibility for what had happened between us; how she sold me as a child; how she allowed my father to sexually abuse me; how their abuse led to a lifetime of loneliness for me. This is what I had done to my father when I killed my mother, leading to a lifetime of longing for her just as I have longed for a partner in this lifetime and that longing has remained unfulfilled. Their actions have created a situation for me so I could repay my karmic debt to them, so I could learn what is feels like to have your life taken away from you. I feel the karmic cycle has ended with me. Forgiveness helped to stop the perpetuation of the cycle. Had I not forgiven her I would be restarting the karmic cycle all over again because I would still be angry with her and would want to take revenge.

Clarity came to me as to why my soul chose these lessons; why my soul chose to be abused by both my father and mother. It was all a karmic energetic cycle that played itself out beautifully so all participants could heal and free themselves from these karmic ties that were causing nothing but suffering in all of us. But I could not see the beauty until I had the readiness and the eyes to see what I had created. This is what it means to be self-realized. It's taking ownership of what you have created. It is accepting your part in all of it. It's about taking responsibility for your part. For me to get to this level of self-acceptance, I had to do the inner child work to strengthen my heart so I could see what I had done. I could not have been a witness to this lifetime had I not done my inner work.

It truly broke my heart to see my own horrible actions that were revealed to me during my journey with the mushrooms. I experienced the depth of my parents' pain. Because this pain was buried so deep, I had to peel off the layers for eleven years before I could get to the core. I saw what I had done to my mother that has made her into who she is today, a narcissist. She also has suffered from myasthenia gravis for the past six years; the disease has attacked the neuromuscular junction of the muscles that move her lungs, making her "air hungry."

My mother has created her own Karma since becoming a narcissist. It is true that hurt people hurt people. In hurting others, we create Karma. Karma doesn't take into account why you did what you did. That is up to the individual to figure out. Karma simply delivers consequences for your actions. I am sure there were other things that contributed to her becoming a narcissist, but I had a big hand in it. Now I must forgive myself for the acts of violence that I have committed against her.

Through this karmic understanding, I could understand why my father molested me. He still carried his desire for me from that past life, when I was his wife. And I still felt my desire to be the only one that he adored. This feeling of desire was no different than the anger and jealousy that my mother and I carried toward each other into this lifetime. When seen from this perspective, did my father truly mistreat me? Or was it simply the unmet desire of two souls? The way I see it, we both chose, at the level of the *soul,* to play out this desire. It is a choice that both of our souls made. I know we have all heard about the soul contracts that we put into place before we incarnate. I speak about it from a place of realizing that I chose this lifetime so that I could clear up this web of energy between the three of us. So that I could stop this karmic cycle from recurring.

The sexual act between my father and me was nothing more than that—a sexual act. My experience with psylocibin allowed me to understand this, and that society's beliefs have not had that same opportunity. What makes it right or wrong is our beliefs around it. I am not saying sex should be permitted between an adult parent and a child. I am asking for understanding into why it happens, and compassion for the souls who bring in these energies into a current lifetime so that they can heal themselves. Because ultimately, it's a soul's journey. The soul does not take into account the physical relationships such as the mother and son or the father and daughter. It is society that creates taboos around relationships as they are perceived to be concrete in this lifetime. The world is called maya or an illusion according to the ancient Hindu scriptures called the Vedas. I share this because this has also been my experience of the world as well. This world changes depending upon which lifetime you are looking at. There is no absolute truth when it comes to our lives and relationships. We are all here role-playing. That is all it is. We can create all the meaning we want to out of it, but ultimately it is role-playing for the growth and evolution of the soul. The only truth is the soul that exists, or the garb a soul wears as an incarnate in the physical reality, does not equal absolute truth.

Our soul is like a multifaceted diamond, The light that is being reflected off the diamond is how many lifetimes a soul is living simultaneously per Theo. If we take a moment to evaluate each lifetime that a soul is living, you will see that a soul plays many different roles so it can learn from them. Who is to say which one is correct? What are we basing societal beliefs and judgments upon? As I said in the introduction, the scenes were ever-evolving and the stage was ever-revolving. The cast is always the same, the characters are different.

I can only share my experience with you in words. Words don't do it justice, yet that is all I have for you now until you begin to experience some of these deeper truths for yourself. My experiences helped me to understand that it's not the sex that causes the trauma to a child but rather the society's limiting beliefs around it. When a child is born, it is born with the belief system of the family, the society, the culture, the race, the religion, the gender, the country, and so on and so forth. So, if the beliefs around sexuality are neutral, there is no trauma that can be created around it. Think of it this way: life is empty and meaningless until we fill it with meaning. Do we have to label it? Must we create conflict around it? Because conflict comes from the ego. Can we simply allow it to be as a society? Neither condemning it nor condoning it. Leaving it be. Not adding any meaning to it. Leave life meaningless. It will lead to less trauma in individuals. Ultimately, as a society we need to take accountability around our limiting beliefs instead of being reactive and learning how they create trauma in others. This is where our evolution lies.

As I've said, this path of emotions is not for the faint of heart. I can warn you that engaging these matters of violence solely with the mind may provoke numerous questions and objections—even anger. Yet, by listening with an open heart, you may uncover the truth. I realize that this will be a trigger for many because the anger of sexual abuse has accumulated in our psyche. Although I seek an alternative understanding of my own situation, I do not condone such violations and crimes against humanity, especially those involving children. I am asking you to take one moment and step outside of your usual perspective. To look at things differently. Consider the opposite. Remember that this is coming from someone who has personally suffered those same crimes. I don't take these acts lightly. I haven't forgotten the suffering I have endured, I say this rather in lieu of the suffering. I have lost a life that I could have lived more fully. Yet I still implore you to think differently. Tune into a greater perspective for the sake of those who are suffering.

This kind of understanding, compassion, and perspective cannot arise from a place of ego. It will arise with the release of judgments, opinions, and beliefs around this topic. You must first open your heart to different perspectives if you truly want to learn.

I couldn't help but think, *what made me do such a thing?* How did I become that cold-blooded murderer? No sooner did I ask the questions than the answers appeared. This one goes back to my older daughter. This event between my older daughter and myself took place during the time of Atlantis. I was a healer during this particular lifetime and my older daughter was my male helper, in whom I trusted completely. Because I trusted him blindly, I didn't see that my helper was jealous of my gifts. One day, he came to my castle and severely abused me, tortured me, raped me, killed me, and then maimed my body.

Because I trusted this man, this came as quite a shock and led to my lack of trust in anyone.

Since then, my current-day daughter and I have had many lifetimes during which we have tortured, raped, sacrificed, and maimed each other. The energies between us have been tumultuous, to say the least. In fact, we had both held onto anger and hatred toward one another, yet the universe brought us together in this lifetime so we could heal it once and for all. Neither one of us could run away from this relationship. We are bound for life. It has forced us to work through our differences.

This reminds me of what Theo taught us. They said that souls tend to incarnate together for sake of growth, and now I got to experience their teaching. A soul chooses which souls it wants to incarnate with based on the opportunity for its greatest growth. I am sure my experience is not the exception, but rather the norm. The universe brings us together so we can learn to heal ourselves. So we can learn to embrace one another in spite of our differences. So we can all experience Love. It is all about Love. Our learning comes from experience. How else can we deepen our understanding of what Love really is?

Awareness of this lifetime has helped me to understand how I became a narcissist. Realizing I was a narcissist could only come from the work that I did, as most narcissists cannot acknowledge their behavior. Our ego is too fragile. It has helped me to see that the traumas I had endured prior to this particular lifetime had made me into the person who killed the king's fourth wife and so many others.

It all started because my soul chose to heal its pattern of blindly trusting others through incurring trauma at the hands of my daughter during the time of Atlantis. Once the trauma occurred, my soul had to clear what it needed to clear to release that particular pattern. It took however long it took to clear it. I had to go through the cascade of domino effects that catapulted me on a healing journey like no other. In its wake there were countless others who were hurt, tortured, and killed. By design this is the process, as I've come to realize.

I know in subsequent lifetimes I have had a heck of a time trusting anyone. It appears my soul went the other way. It went from blindly trusting everyone to not trusting anyone. The pendulum had to swing the other way to bring back the balance. It had to be a journey of TRUST because that is what I needed to learn to balance. It could not have gone down any other way. That is why Theo guided me to "TRUST" as an action step during one of our classes. I understand now what they were conveying twelve years ago and what my soul has been trying to accomplish for thousands of lifetimes!

Needless to say, these insights and realizations have allowed me to forgive my mother and father. This process has helped me to have a better relationship with my daughter. This is alchemy at its best. I went from hating my mom to asking her for forgiveness, all because I had a new perspective on why she did what she did. The situation completely turned around. I was no longer angry with her, but instead felt remorse at my own actions more than a thousand years later. Of course, I have not shared any of this with her as I am not sure she will understand or that she is ready to look at it.

In the end I can tell you this, that I didn't need to go to a medical school to create alchemy. No amount of research would have led me to these insights. Had I spent my time reading through every available article in western medical journals, I would still be searching. My time is precious, and I will not waste it on reading useless material that does nothing for my soul. I simply had to have the courage to turn within when everyone around me was looking without. It is a simple shift in perception that opened the doorways to my mental health.

I have come full circle. I am learning to trust with discernment. I am putting up boundaries where boundaries are needed. I have transcended my narcissism and can now think and make decisions from my heart instead of the mind. My mind has become the servant to my heart. It is a great feeling to have accomplished this enormous task. If I can do it, so can you.

I now understand that the trauma I had endured made me into the person I had become when I killed my mom in a previous lifetime. The pain inflicted on my mother turned her into the person that she is today. It is a domino effect that we cannot escape until we make a conscious choice to do our inner work. This is the power of inner child work, this is the power of self-Love.

All the information taught in medical school will be obsolete soon because there would be no need for it if you turn within and tap into the powers that lie dormant within you to heal yourself, without waiting years and years for a research study to come out that might deliver abysmal results at best. There are many healers who can heal simply with a touch. No knowledge is required for that. It doesn't matter whether it's acute or chronic. This has not been your experience because that's what you believe. Remember the universe delivers what you believe in. Someone once asked Theo why he couldn't fly. Theo responded by asking, "Do you believe you can fly?" Also, Jesus could raise from the dead. What do you think he used? My guess is energy. What drug do you know of that can raise from the dead? Having studied medicine and countless research articles, I can tell you I don't know of any. Yet you put so much faith in western medicine and none in energy and none in yourself and your ability to heal yourself. Jesus also went on to say, "You too can do what I can do and more." Why are we not taught how to cultivate the powers that are contained within us? But I suppose you can wait for another study to give you the permission to turn within for your healing. Or you can begin to trust.

The good news is that creating alchemy is quite simple, and the healing is instantaneous once you learn how to do it. Simplicity does not equate to ease. To learn to create shifts in energy, you must first realize that you are responsible for creating your illness. The moment you take on the responsibility, you become empowered to change it. When you can see how you've created an illness, you will know how to shift it.

As you can see, you are not going to find your health at a doctor's office or in a medical journal. This is not to say to not go see a doctor, but rather to remember that you are the healer that you are looking for. You can get the diagnosis and even the recommended treatment, but remember that only you can heal yourself. There is nothing and no one outside of you who can do that for you.

And it all began with the ABCs of spirituality. In my case, it started with tuning into the Voice that was arising from within me. It started with recognizing the Voice, by trusting the Voice, by listening to it. I began to spend hours in solitude, leaving my husband to care for my daughters while I dedicated some time to communing with the Voice.

The challenge was to trust the Voice because I was so used to ignoring it. Some of the things that it was telling me to do were difficult on one hand, but I knew it would be liberating in the end. I followed the trail to liberation. As you start this work you will notice the urge to negate the Voice, as it will not appease your ego. It will test your foundational beliefs. It will bring to the surface all that you have shoved under the rug and have you reexamine it.

The more you do the inner child work, the more you will be able to discern whose voice it is that you are hearing. Is it the voice of the ego or is it the Voice of the spirit? You will also have more strength and courage to follow the Voice. The more whole you become, the deeper your healing will be. Let your illness be your motivation to do your inner work, because your physical illness is a symptom of deeper issues. It is letting you know that there is something you need to heal. A hole you need to sew. A tear in the fabric of your being that you need to mend. It is your friend in disguise. Lean into it. Allow it to teach you what it's here to teach you.

Chapter 5

The Karmic Predicament

No one is free of Karma unless you are enlightened, and even then, a certain kind of Karma stays with you. The inner child work will help you to clear Karma. It will help you to see things as they are, not as you want them to be or as you *think* they are. We all have a veil of forgetfulness as an act of compassion. If you knew what you have done to others in your past lives, you may not be able to look at yourself in the mirror. You will see that you have cast stones before and will not be able to handle it. To handle the enormity of your actions, you need to begin by first creating a distance between you and your ego. Because you, the soul, are not your ego. Your soul thinks it's the ego but it's not. Inner child work will help you to see the divine being that you are. It will help you to create a distance between you and your ego. You will begin to feel the essence of our soul. You will be able to recognize it with your consciousness.

Ego is simply patterns of thoughts that run your life. Ego is not the real you. It is the "made up" version of you. As I alluded to earlier, ego is the lower mind. The lower mind is formed when the mind is split as a result of the trauma. The particular segment of the mind that gets split has its own set of beliefs.

These beliefs are formed for the sake of survival. For instance, a child whose father is loving by the day but becomes abusive while drinking at night may form the belief, "Those who love you will hurt you." The belief is formed as a defense mechanism so the child can be on the lookout and protect herself by not over trusting and staying out of her father's way when he is drunk, granted she is old enough to do that. As an adult this child will have difficulty having intimate relationships if she continues to hold onto this belief. She will find a partner who is loving at times and abusive at other times. This pattern will continue until she releases this particular belief. Because when we have a belief, our mind will create a situation to prove to itself the validity of the belief. The inner child work helps us to release limiting beliefs by integrating the lower mind back into the higher mind. The integration process helps you to realize that you are not your ego. That you are a divine being.

Once you begin to become disidentified with the ego then you will be able to face your sins. The word sin comes from the word sine. It simply means to miss the mark. You will be able to see where you missed the mark without judging yourself harshly for it. This is the process of evolution for the soul. The soul learns by going through lessons which can take thousands of years, hence the recycling of the soul. For instance, if you have never had a cut on your finger, how would you know what it feels like to have a cut on your finger? How would you know how painful it is? This is why we have all role-played as the rapist and the one who has been raped. We have all been the murderer and the victim. I just happen to remember the crimes that I have committed in the past. You are no different. Those souls who have gone through the lessons are ready to awaken. To awaken to the teachings within the lessons.

When you do the inner child work you will feel the grief of what could have been. In essence what you are doing is feeling the pain of someone who has been through the same situation as you. When you feel the emotional pain of what you have been through that's what is called awakening. You are awakening to your feelings! When you are not so numb to your feelings, you will begin to understand the consequences of your actions toward another. You will think twice before your act. You will no longer be so reactionary. This is how you will build compassion.

An awakened soul is a compassionate soul. The lessons you go through will teach you compassion only if you are able to tune into the feelings that lie behind the lessons. The lessons are about learning what it's like to be on both ends of the stick, so to speak. All of the masters, such as Jesus, Mother Mary, and Kuan Yin, are extremely compassionate. Kuan Yin is known as the goddess of compassion. That's because they have gone through the cycle of life and learned their lessons just as we are doing. This is why only you will know whether you have learned what you wanted to learn and are now ready to awaken to your divinity. When we step into our Masterhood is when our gifts emerge, such as the ability to heal ourselves.

To build compassion toward another we must first release judgments toward ourselves. We often judge others so harshly because we have the same energetic pattern in our energy field but cannot face that within ourselves, so we project that judgment or anger onto another person. The reason we cannot face it is because we are judging ourselves harshly. You will notice that when you begin to release judgment toward yourself through inner child work, you will soften. What angers you about another person won't trigger you anymore. You won't have to "control" your anger because there will be nothing there. You will begin to feel more and more at peace. This is the power of inner child work.

Once you start to release harsh judgments toward the self, the universe will unveil what you need to work with next, and the truth will surface from the veil of existence. Once the veil lifts, you will be able to have a better understanding of Karma. That's when you will begin to tap into the mysteries of the universe. You will understand the inner workings of the universe for yourself. You will begin to make sense of the ratchet of all the reactions that drive this universe. Having a working knowledge of how the universe operates will help you to navigate through it and perhaps even help you to stay motivated on this path. Because it is your sheer will that will get you through to the other side. You won't need a "guru" to explain to you what the universe is like. You will see the truth behind it for yourself once and for all.

Being born into a Sikh family in India, I was taught the basics of Karma. Twenty-four years of working as a physician has shown me how Karma affects the physical body. The twelve years of inner child work has shown me how the cogwheels of Karma turn even between lifetimes to bring about an illness in this lifetime. Death does not stop their churning. Death does not forgive our karmic debts. Death does not forge our karmic signature. Death recycles the soul, so we have a chance at redo. It gives us a different body with the same thought patterns. It gives us another chance to do things differently.

I call this the Groundhog Effect, based on the movie *Groundhog Day*, in which the character of Bill Murray experiences the same day over and over until he chooses differently. In this case, it is the same *Groundhog Day* life until you choose differently. The power of choice can break us free from the cycle of Karma, as I will explain in more detail later.

This is all delegated by the Law of Karma (LOK). LOK decides what kind of a body the soul will have. It determines what kind of lessons a soul will go through, depending upon what it needs to learn. As they say, it is the same shit, different life. There truly is no escaping your lessons. This is how a soul grows. This is how a soul evolves. This is how a soul is lightened of the karmic burdens of pains it has caused another over the span of lifetimes. The pain we cause another leads to a heavy heart laden with guilt and even self-loathing for the actions we may have committed. We begin to hate ourselves for what we have done to others. Hence the sense of unworthiness that we all have.

The only way to release the guilt is to feel the pain that we have caused another. It is to feel it and to release it. This is why we choose certain lessons. These lessons lead to emotional pain, which then fragments the soul. To integrate the fragmented part of our soul, we have to feel the emotional pain that caused the split even in a different lifetime. That's why my previous life as a child who was sacrificed emerged when I was feeling stuck on my spiritual journey. I couldn't move forward until I dealt with the pain from that lifetime.

As I mentioned earlier, to feel this emotional pain and release it you need an emotional body. We get the emotional body only when we have a physical body, which means we cannot process these emotions in any other realm. This can only happen in this physical realm. So, use your time here on earth wisely. Because if you don't, you may be back for a take—16,034 in my case.

The soul may choose to release this guilt in a variety of ways. One way is to give birth to someone whose life you may have taken in a past life, as in the case of me and my older daughter. In one of our past lifetimes, we were partners. She was the man, and I was the woman. In that lifetime, she was abusive toward me and bullied me to a point where she had me cornered. I was scared and didn't know how to free myself, so I ended up killing her. To give her back the life I had taken, I had to give birth to her in this lifetime. It has been quite fascinating for me to witness how the roles and even the gender were switched for my daughter. Since my daughter overpowered me, as a man in our previous lifetime together, she incarnated not only as a woman (so she could feel what it's like to be overpowered by someone) but as my child, making me an authority figure whom she had to rely upon for her survival. Quite the humbling position, I feel. There is a lesson in each and every role we play. The soul chooses perfectly each time. As Theo once said, "The soul is not stupid." The Karma is played out with such precision that it has left me in awe of the divine orchestration and intervention.

Another way I cleared Karma was to take on the abuse as I did as a child because I felt guilty about what I had done to my mother in another life. All of the information unraveled slowly as I did my inner child work. It came in the way of one realization at a time. In fact, that's how I knew that I was integrating into my wholeness. The more I integrated, the more the deeper layers surfaced in order to be seen. The Voice would slowly reveal the secrets when I was ready to look at them without judging myself harshly. I don't think I could have handled the enormity of these revelations all at once. It's as if my energy were tied up in a knot that unraveled slowly over time as I did my inner work. There were times when I could feel a fluttering in my brain as new neuronal connections formed there. This reminds me of a quote by Rumi, "Seek the wisdom that will untie your knot. Seek the path that demands your whole being."

How you pay off Karma is dependent on a lot of different factors, such as who is involved, the dynamics of how the Karma was created, and also the soul's mission in life. In my case I was in a major karmic predicament with both of my parents and my older daughter. This was a lot of Karma to clear. My mission in this lifetime was to free myself of the rest of the pending Karma so I could be released from the cycle of reincarnation. And I did so by taking on enormous amount of pain.

It is not necessarily an eye-for-an-eye type of retribution all the time. It's about the lesson. The soul chooses how it can repay the karmic debt. Had I chosen to be murdered by my mother in this lifetime I would have not been able to repay the Karma that I had created with my father, because by killing my mom I'd sentenced my father to a life of pain and separation. By choosing to be born to my parents and choosing the life that I chose, which included being sexually abused at the hands of both my father and mother, I lived a life of isolation, loneliness, poverty, and the pain that comes with it. In spite of being an MD in the United States, I have lost everything, including my childhood and my innocence. I had to ask my parents for financial support at the age of fifty-four. There came a point when I could not even afford rent. Not to mention the enormous amount of debt I incurred in this process. Karma brought me to my knees and turned me into a beggar. Such is the justice of Karma. When it comes for you, watch out! I feel by taking on the enormous amount of pain that I have in this lifetime, the karmic scales have been balanced. Justice has been served by the lords of Karma.

I want to follow this up by saying that I chose to leave my job as a conventional medicine practitioner. I chose to go through the hardships so that I could clear my Karma. I could simply have stayed at my job and made plenty of money. That would have likely meant coming back in another lifetime to pay off my Karma. We have free will. We can choose to exercise our free will when we want. Having said that, I don't really know what would have happened had I not chosen the path of liberation. I can only speculate.

One would think that since I killed my mom in a previous lifetime, I would have had to give birth to her to pay off my Karma just as I had to do with my daughter. But that was not the case. Even though I did not give birth to my mother, I still gave up the first fifty some years of my life. Because of the severity of the abuse, I had a personality disorder. People like me end up in psych wards and correctional facilities. We can't make friends and keep them. It is an extremely lonely and arduous road. Most of my life was spent in confusion and dissociation, completely unaware and unconscious of my surroundings.

Because of the abuse, I had a cognitive brain dysfunction, which meant that I could not make good decisions for myself. I was lost in life. I ended up eloping with a married Sikh priest. As Sikhs we are not allowed to cut our hair, so when we eloped, we both cut our hair in hopes that we would not be identified. By taking such actions I disgraced my family and the Sikh tradition. For this, I was ostracized from my family and isolated myself from the community, owing to my own shame around my actions. To make things worse, the man I married isolated me from my friends as well. He was emotionally unavailable and a narcissist who was abusive and controlling both to me and our daughters. Sadly, every man I've met since my divorce has also been abusive in some way, shape, or form. How could I attract a healthy partner when I had a personality disorder and had created Karma around separating a couple from each other when I killed my mom in a past life?

My graduation from med school was also a way to repay my Karma. It was a way out of suffering. I was given a choice. If I served humanity, then my suffering would be alleviated considerably. I believe that I was given a chance to go to med school so I could redeem my Karma through service to humanity. I believe it's because I had this contract with God that I am being relieved from loneliness, poverty, and sickness. I believe this book is part of the contract I had with God to help me clear my Karma, and in return I will serve humanity to the best of my ability. This contract is my destiny. I could not have stepped into this destiny without first doing the inner child work and clearing my Karma the best I could.

These are only a few different ways of how I am serving my time here on earth. There are many other ways to clear Karma, and they include early death, illness, pain, being killed, being raped, and a multitude of other ways that are difficult to fathom. Everything in our life serves a purpose to help us to awaken to our destiny. But we can't see the bigger purpose until we embark on this journey; only then will certain things be revealed to us.

Karma is simply a cause and effect. It is a way of learning that your actions have a consequence. While in this case it was perceived to be "bad," it is not always bad. There is also good Karma. Unfortunately, both good and bad Karma keep you stuck in the cycle of reincarnation or death and rebirth. The goal of a lifetime is to not create any new Karma while clearing old Karma. The way to not create more Karma, good or bad, is through heart-based thoughts, words, and actions. The whole point of a lifetime is to break that cycle. In India, it is the cultural norm to want to break the cycle of reincarnation.

The cycle of reincarnation is a painful one. Imagine being in your mother's uterus for nine months, drinking your own pee and smelling the poop and pee of your mother, curled up in a tight ball where there is nothing but darkness, waiting to be cooked to perfection before you can exit the womb through a teeny tiny hole where every bit of fluid is being squeezed out of your lungs so you can breathe when you come out. It is a difficult process both for the mother and the baby. Same thing is true for when you are dying. Not being able to breathe and not knowing when that last inhale will come. The anticipation is pure agony. Not to mention the suffering that we endure while living this life.

This is why the monks and the sadhus devote a lifetime to trying to attain moksha or liberation. Liberation from what? Liberation from the cycle of death and rebirth, liberation from suffering, liberation from mental constructs that we have created that create a loop in our thought patterns, which in turn keep us stuck in the cycle of reincarnation. This is why the seers and sages aim for enlightenment. Enlightenment is enlightening of the heart of our soul.

Even if we create Karma in our ignorance, the Law of Karma does not excuse ignorance. So, let's learn about different types of Karma so we can learn to steer through it and relieve our hearts from the burdens of Karma.

There are three different types of Karma:

1. Prarabdha

2. Sanchita

3. Agami

Prarabdha – the word "prarab" comes from Sanskrit, and it means to begin. The word prarabdha in relation to Karma means "action that has begun." In the meaning of the word lies the description. It means that the Karma is in action; it is in motion. The analogy I can give you is similar to when a bow leaves the arrow. The bow is in motion and cannot be retrieved at that point.

An example is when I gave birth to my daughter, I set the Karma in motion. Once she was born, I could not stop the events from unfolding the way they unfolded. This included my anger toward her and my treatment of her even as an infant, which was not nurturing.

This Karma will likely be done in one lifetime because a certain amount of karmic debt is set into motion so the debt can be cleared. The soul gets to choose how much debt it wants to clear in a particular lifetime.

While there is no way to stop the flow, you can certainly stop the Ping-Pong match in this lifetime through the process of forgiveness. When you forgive, the karmic arrow stops with you. You do not have to throw the arrow back to the other person. But you can only do this if you forgive. Otherwise, the force of Karma to act on your desire to harm someone is very strong. Karma acts like a magnet attracting you to each other. Forgiveness is an act of self-Love.

Sanchita – this word means "piled up" in Sanskrit. In relation to Karma, it means "action that has piled up." This is Karma in latency. As long as you have piled up Karma, you will have the desire to reincarnate to pay off your karmic debt. Because the soul feels guilty about what it has done, it incarnates in hopes of being able to repent its actions. Even though the soul's desire is to repent for its karmic actions, it is still pushed by the karmic forces when it incarnates. It has to do its inner work to be able to forgive and stop the volley of Karma.

The beauty of this Karma is that it has not been set in motion yet, which means you can clear it by doing the inner child work. The bow has not yet left the arrow, which means you can halt the cycle of reincarnation.

Repentance clears the latent Karma. When you feel remorseful about your actions, you actually feel the pain that you caused another. You are putting yourself in their shoes and feeling their pain.

The reason we experience pain is so that we can learn from it, so we can grow from it. As I mentioned earlier, how would you know what it feels like to be violated unless you were violated yourself? When you do your inner child work it will reveal to you what you did to another. When we become aware of the consequences of our actions then we can feel that same pain that we inflicted on another person and then release this pain. Through feeling this pain, you are saying to the universe that you have learned what it feels like to be in that person's shoes. Since you already know what the pain feels like, you don't have to go through the karmic steps or situations that would have inflicted that pain on you for you to be able to feel it. The universe then relieves you of your Karma.

Agami – It means "waiting" in Sanskrit. In relation to Karma, it means "waiting to act." This is present-day action that has a future consequence. On this journey, it is not only important to clear previously created Karma, but it is equally important to not create imprints for new Karma that you will be responsible for in a future lifetime(s).

This is where Karma can be a bit tricky, because both good and bad Karma will keep you on the hamster wheel of reincarnation. The only way out is through your heart. When your thoughts, words, and actions are in alignment with your heart, you will stop generating new Karma.

Ram Dass gives a beautiful example of heart-based thoughts, words, and actions. Say there is a man dying on the floor, and you decide to save this man. A week later, when the man is feeling better, he gets up and goes and kills someone. That Karma is on you as well because you helped to save the man who committed a murder.

The Voice is saying that had you been in touch with your heart, your heart would have told you not to save the man. But your mind would likely trick you with its commentary about how selfish you are for not wanting to save this man. Or how bad you are because you are now responsible for killing this man. Its constant commentary is pure torture. And if you didn't save the man, it will repeatedly make you feel guilty about not saving this man. Its unrelenting chatter will not let you live a life of peace to a point where you wished you had saved the man.

The only way to rise above mind chatter is to drop into your heart. Allow the heart to be the king that it is. However, you cannot do that when your heart is heavy and ridden with guilt. This burden of guilt keeps your king off its throne, while the mind takes over and runs your life. The inner child work is the thread that will mend your heart. It will sew together the pieces of your tattered heart. The God-Self within you will bring it back to life! Your enlightened heart will lead you out of the maze of reincarnation.

What I have realized is that being the savior is not always a good thing, contrary to the popular belief, contrary to the societal chimes to "always be kind" without really knowing what it means to be kind. In this case an act of kindness is to let the man die so that you can save an innocent person's life. You will not be able to understand this unless you know how to listen to your heart and listen with your heart. Because when you come from the heart, even in your anger there will be love. Even in your anger there would be kindness. Even in your anger there would be compassion. Even in your anger there would be protection. Your anger will be your act of love. You will be able to understand what I am saying if you listen to the Voice of the heart and not the chattering of the mind.

This journey we call life is teaching us the ways of the heart. It is important to be able to discern the Voice of the heart from the voice in your head. To operate from the heart, you have to heal your broken heart so that your heart can take its rightful place as the king that it is and allow the mind to take its rightful place as a servant that it is.

I had been doing the inner child work for about ten years. This helped me to open my heart enough that it was time for my sexual healing, because I still couldn't breathe the same air as a man. My whole body would tense up when I would so much as see a man. My brain would stop thinking. I would feel awkward in the presence of a man, making it impossible to have any kind of conversation with a man, let alone a relationship.

I was guided to travel to Colombia to visit a friend who had experience with sexual healing. She introduced me to a tantric healer. He spent the first three hours trying to get me to simply look at him. I was so ashamed of my desires that I could not even look at him. That's when I realized that I had a lot of work to do still when it came to healing my sexuality. Something so pleasurable had become my shadow, something I was very ashamed of.

The Voice shared with me the importance of healing all parts of me, and this included my sexuality. I also felt that this leg of the journey would be a difficult one. Not that it had been easy up until that point. Upon my return back home to the USA, I met a guy who was to be my partner in the sexual healing process. He introduced me to psychedelics, namely LSD and psilocybin. The Voice began to show me how to work with the psychedelics in a sacred ceremonial way. It would tell me when to take, what to take, and how much to take. It would also teach me how to work with the medicine so I could heal from the trauma. It was always low amounts, and I never took them unless instructed by the Voice.

I remember one particular day, we had been working together for about six months when my partner told me that he was going to be triggering me. *No big deal,* I thought, because by now I had been doing the inner child work for ten years. I guess I was wrong. He did a phenomenal job, I might add. He was guided to have sex with a gal who was much younger than me and was staying with me for a couple of months. All three of us sat down and discussed what we were all feeling needed to happen, and we realized that we were all receiving the same guidance, and we all consented.

The following evening, he proceeded to have sex with her right in front of me. Even though we were sexual healing partners and not romantic partners, to witness him do that was extremely painful. I thought I was going to lose my mind. He inflicted a deep pain in my heart. In fact, the pain was so intense that I felt just beside myself. I couldn't bear the thought of it, let alone see it. His hunger for her deepened the pain even more so. I went into a state of panic. I didn't know what to do or think. Was this some kind of a joke? I felt enraged at their actions even though there had been a prior discussion.

I was guided by the Voice to heal the pain using LSD. The following evening, I decided to journey with LSD. I locked myself in my bedroom and went under. As the LSD began to take over, it intensified the emotional pain. Then it showed me that the pain my healing partner had inflicted penetrated my heart like an arrow. The arrow went in from the front of my heart and came out the back of my heart, aiming for the back of my partner's heart coming out of the front of his heart and coming back to me. This arrow created a loop. It was showing me that the pain he had inflicted was karmic. My desire to hurt him as much as he had hurt me kept the loop going. My desire to hurt him was the propelling force behind the motion of this karmic arrow.

If I hurt him, he would have the desire to hurt me, and the cycle would perpetuate itself. Then it went on to show me that we would have to reincarnate together for eternity because we were both stuck in this karmic loop. I certainly did not want to be tied to this fella or anyone, for that matter, for eternity. So, I asked for a solution. As soon as I asked for a solution, I heard the words, "Love yourself." *Well, how on earth is that going to help my situation?* I thought. But I didn't have much of a choice. I began to tell myself that I love myself, even though I didn't want to say it and certainly didn't believe in it. But I said it anyway. At first nothing happened, but slowly as I repeated the mantra, "I love myself anyway, many ways, all ways," I began to feel physical pressure on the left side of my chest. Then I felt an energetic valve flip from a vertical position to horizontal position. As soon as the valve flipped horizontal, it fell on the hole in my heart created by the arrow as if patching it and allowed the flow of self-love to begin. It was coming somewhere from the left side of my heart. I had never experienced this flow before, and it has not stopped.

I had not realized that because we don't love ourselves that the valve gets stuck in a closed position, and we have to work toward opening it. Self-Love is the key to stopping the karmic cycle of death and rebirth. But to open the valve of self-love, I had to first open my heart with the inner child work. Self-Love stopped the karmic loop, and it took only one person to free both of us from reincarnating together lifetime after lifetime to inflict pain on one another. When you Love yourself, you lose all desire to hurt another.

The purpose of creating this situation was twofold. First, to show me how Karma works. Second, to show me that the deep pain my partner had elicited was an attachment wound I already carried within me. That's why his actions produced an unbearable emotional pain. His actions were more like the salt on the wound. When I felt this pain and loved myself in the face of it, it helped me to heal that deep place of wounding. This is when I realized that had I not been emotionally wounded as a child, his actions would not have created Karma to begin with. This is why it is important to heal from these emotional wounds that we all carry. It was a painful, yet a necessary step in my spiritual evolution. As you can see, trust is an important ingredient in this work.

The inner child work will clear Karma from all lifetimes, not just this one. Whatever you are being presented with in this lifetime is your guide as to where you need to clear Karma for the most part. If you have a karmic imprint that needs to be cleared, but you don't have any awareness of it because it's from another lifetime, then you will have a recall of that lifetime so that you can clear it. For the most part all that you need to clear is right here in front of you. If and when you need to be reminded of another lifetime that you need to clear, that information will be revealed to you. This is where you trust the universe to guide the process. The more you do your inner work, the more you will begin to know the process. The more you will begin to connect the dots. Our destinies are as grand as we are. All of our souls desire to be of significance. We all want to experience the pinnacle of peace, joy, and abundance that is our birthright. To get to that level of manifestation you must first clear your Karma through repentance and self-Love. Yes, you can compartmentalize some of your emotions to manifest success in this physical plane, such as in finances, relationships, and physical health, but the mysteries of the universe are only open to those who forgive and love themselves.

Once you come out on the other side, the world will be your oyster. You will know who you are at your core. There will be no derailing you. You will remain steadfast in your mission, working toward your destiny.

Had I not gone down the road to self-discovery with the inner child work, I would not have seen my part in the relationship and would not have forgiven my mother. We would have both carried those energies into another lifetime and perhaps attempted to hurt each other again. I would not only have lived a life of adversity in this lifetime but would have set myself up to do the same in another lifetime, bathing myself with guilt, anger, violence, and suffering. I Love myself enough that I don't have any desire for revenge toward anyone.

I believe that in this lifetime my soul chose to walk the path of healing and forgiveness. Once you act in a manner that creates Karma, then you get stuck in a karmic loop, and it becomes a Ping-Pong match. In any given lifetime, we have a choice. We can continue to react and keep the karmic match alive, or we can choose to put down our arrow and not pierce another's heart.

Chapter 6

Secure Attachment with Yourself

OUR RELATIONSHIPS ARE THE KEY to our health. Health is not just physical as conventional medicine would have you believe. Health begins with a healthy mind that thinks healthy, positive thoughts. A healthy mind will not just create a healthy body but also a healthy life, because thoughts are our primary nutrition and form the soil for our health. When soil is formed with unadulterated energy, the plant of health will blossom unapologetically. You will find health in your finances. You will find health in your relationships. You will find health in all that you do. Because it's your thoughts that create your reality, and higher thoughts come from the divine source for which the mind is a vehicle. However, healthy thoughts cannot be transmitted when the mind is fractured.

When trauma happens, it causes the mind to split, and the imprint of that trauma gets stored in the mind, and you can't help but think certain thoughts over and over again. Negative thoughts come from the lower mind that has split, just as the soul is split with trauma. This means that the soil is formed with energy that has been foiled. When you have a split mind, the plant of health will not blossom, no matter how many doctors you see. No matter how many medications you take. No matter how many surgeries you have. Any sense of wellness you may get is deceptive at best because it's your thoughts that create your health, not your doctors or the medications you take. Any thought that you think for longer than seventeen seconds will manifest in your physical reality. As long as it's your split mind that has short-circuited and is thinking the thoughts, you will not be able to create a healthy life.

When you think certain thoughts repeatedly, they form a track in your brain and psyche. It's similar to the ski tracks that get imprinted in the snow with repeated use. In a similar manner, these thoughts form tracks in your brain and psyche over time. The older you get, the harder it becomes to change these thought patterns, leading to irreversible damage to the psyche, manifesting in mental illness.

The foundation for mental health is formed during childhood. The kind of childhood we have determines the kind of adulthood we will have. Our childhood imprints our adulthood. Sadly, our current societal and familial structure breeds trauma. How caregivers relate to their child determines the kind of bond the child will form with their caregiver, which will have a lifelong impact on the child and will determine how healthy a child will be as an adult. If we, as adults, are unable to heal the trauma, it comes with us into our next life. This is how trauma gets layered; hence, it comes off in layers like an onion.

Attachment styles are fundamental to the kind of relationships we will have as an adult. The kind of relationship we have with our parents is the kind of partner we will attract in our intimate relationships. Given how many adults struggle with intimate relationships and how it affects our health, I feel this is an important topic of discussion.

We know that our relationships impact our physical health in particular. Dysfunctional relationships affect heart health, gut health, endocrine system, circulatory system, immune system, and much more.

Attachment styles can be seen early on as they are being formed. We can spot them if we are astute parents. Then again, if we are astute parents, we won't have a child with insecure attachment to begin with.

We arrived in Chandigarh from Delhi, India. It was about a seven-hour bus ride. I was a little more than two years old. My dad's sister had taken me and her two sons from Delhi to Chandigarh to visit her mom. My mom had stayed behind. This is a vague memory, but I remember I needed to go poop. For some reason I didn't want to. I don't know why, but I was trying to hold it back. I did my best to not go. It had been two days of my holding my poop in, and my aunt was worried. Somehow, she could tell that I was withholding it. So, she decided to take me back to my mom. She got on the bus back to Delhi. As soon as we got back, I took a big dump! "I knew it," she said. Then I remember the two of them laughing at how I just wouldn't poop. My aunt tells this story to this day.

I now believe that withholding poop was a form of power struggle that stemmed from the disorganized attachment style that I had. I wanted to be close to my mom because I felt like I could not bond with her. Not pooping was my way of saying I want to be near my mom. It was something I could control temporarily, anyway.

Over the years, I've been told stories of how I was very clingy as a child. That when my mom would hold me, I would not allow anyone else to hold me. I have also been told that when my mom hit me and I would cry, she was the only one who could console me. I felt and remember this push and pull within me, because this push and pull also played a role in my adult relationships. I remember wanting my mom to console me, yet I didn't want to go to her when she did. I wanted her to beg me not to be mad at her. It would take her a long time to be able to comfort me. Even when she did, I still felt hurt and angry with her. I was never completely satisfied with my connection with my mama.

As an adult when I felt hurt by someone, I wanted the other person to beg me for forgiveness. I felt the same anger toward them as I did toward my mom. At that moment, the person was no longer my friend or partner but rather my mother. Imagine wanting your intimate partner to beg you for forgiveness? What kind of a relationship would you have with that person?

Patterns such as this don't just resolve with time. There is no serendipitous cure. You have to work at releasing these ingrained patterns. They don't just go away; in fact, they affect every relationship you have, especially the one you have with your inner child. Understanding attachment styles is necessary for parenting your inner child.

The more you can become aware and understand these styles, the more compassion you will have for the predicament that you are in, and the quicker you will be able to help your inner child to sidestep the roadblocks along the way.

Why do we attach to begin with? In a nutshell, our survival depends on it. It is a primal need. This helps us to know who we can turn to for sustenance. It provides a sense of security. It gives a sense of belongingness. This is especially important when we are newborns.

As the child is conceived it begins to attach to its carrier. Then as the child is born it begins to attach to its caregiver. According to attachment theory, which concerns relationships between humans, there are two different attachment styles.

1. Secure attachment

2. Insecure attachment

In my personal experience, I have found truth in this theory. It resonated deeply within me when I began to study this theory and saw how it has played out in my life. It helped me to understand how I've come to be who I am. It has connected so many dots to things that made no sense to me. It helped me to develop compassion for myself. It has helped me to have a deeper insight into my behavior. It helped me to comprehend why it has been so difficult for me to have relationships. It helped me to see why my relationships have been so tumultuous.

Secure attachment occurs when all of the child's physical and emotional needs are met appropriately and consistently. It usually happens when the biological mother is able to be present with the child and is responsive to the child's needs in an appropriate time,

According to the Center for Anxiety Disorders, if a child is adopted, he will have abandonment issues and no matter how good his adoptive caregiver is, he will struggle with issues of abandonment and won't be able to form a secure attachment until he can heal himself through self-reflection and inner child work. While there are a plethora of studies that exist that have noted this to be the case, I derived this conclusion simply by doing the inner child work. This elicits that the answers are truly within us, as Buddha said.

People with secure attachments have a healthy life. They are not stuck in their lower mind with negative thoughts. Secure attachment also provides a sense of safety. When you are not in a survival mode, it is much easier to create. Creative thoughts can flow through you. When you are worried about who might abandon you at any given moment, then you go into survival mode. It's hard to relax and allow the creative juices to flow through you. When you feel secure, you have healthy and trusting intimate relationships. Those with this style approach relationships with confidence, openness, and respect. These people also have a positive outlook on life.

Insecure attachment: This attachment style occurs when the child's physical and or emotional needs are not met appropriately. This can happen when the caregiver is either physically or emotionally unavailable, or both. How many adults do you know who are unavailable, whether it's physical or emotional, who are raising children? Almost every family that I know of has both parents working. The feminist movement has broken our homes. It has created dysfunction in our families and communities. It has torn the very fabric and foundation of relationships. When parents cannot be available, it puts the child in fear. Fear of being abandoned. Fear of being rejected. Fear of its very survival. The child begins to develop a lack of trust in not only the caregiver, but their environment. It perceives its environment, hence the world, as unsafe and hostile, which then makes the child act out in ways that reflect his or her inner turmoil. The child then lives its life as an adult who struggles to feel safe, which lends to a life lived in fear rather than Love. Our mode of operation becomes fear instead of Love. Part of the journey entails rewiring your nervous system to feel safe so you can come from a place of love rather than fear.

I have recollection of memories from when I was in my mother's womb. These memories are stored in the body, not in the brain, as the brain has not developed enough to be able to store memories while in utero. Kids who are adopted certainly feel abandoned even though they cannot consciously recall the memory. I feel it is the absence of the biological mother that triggers the abandonment wound and likely leads to anxious attachment style at a minimum.

There are three kinds of insecure attachments.

1. Anxious

2. Avoidant

3. Disorganized

Anxious Attachment Style: This attachment style happens when the caregiver is unpredictable. Because of the inconsistency, you never know when you are going to be dropped like a hot potato. The problem that this creates is that the child is not willing to separate from their caregiver in an attempt to form the bond.

As an adult this attachment style manifested as neediness in many areas of my life but especially with my husband. I over-gave constantly, not leaving any room to be able to receive. My husband and I were constantly together. We didn't need space from each other. When we first started our marriage, we were inseparable. We were together almost all the time. Even when he went to work, I would go to his work and just sit around and wait for him to get done. I could not imagine being alone even for a moment. My desire to form a connection was very strong; so much so that I felt very jealous even when he spoke to his female coworker. I was jealous when he gave anyone else more attention than he gave me. It felt like he was taking something away from me. I was extremely possessive of him as he was of me. I was constantly worried that he might leave me for his coworker who was a beautiful young woman.

We smothered each other and thought we were in love. We constantly fought over his coworker, and I needed constant reassurance he wouldn't leave me for her.

The way our relationship started out was that he pursued me for four months before I finally said yes. At first, when he asked me out, I did not want to go out with him. He would call me up to thirty-plus times a day some days to try to convince me to go out with him. I felt so special and flattered. I took it as a sign of love. I loved the attention that I was getting from him as I was starving for it.

This is what I used to fantasize about. He was my prince charming. I thought this was healthy. I thought this was how it was all supposed to go down. This was normal to my trauma-tized brain.

Avoidant attachment style*:* This attachment style happens when a child does not receive the care and attention that they need to develop a healthy bond with their caregiver. In this style, the caregiver is neglectful and outright abusive. The child feels rejected when he or she is abused. This pain of rejection is greater than the pain of not attaching to the caregiver. So, the child begins to distance himself or herself emotionally from the caregiver. He or she begins to avoid the caregiver.

As an adult I had difficulty talking about my feelings; a sense of being overwhelmed would overcome me. When I felt hurt by someone, I felt frazzled and ashamed, so I would com-pletely cut off the relationship. I did this to many people over the years. When I initially formed relationships, I would think that the person is so nice and would often want to become their best friend the moment I met them.

I had no idea that there was such a thing as social cues. I often overshared with strangers, hoping to gain their trust. This was my way of bonding with someone. I often walked away thinking we had a great connection, only to never hear from them again. I was blind to their reactions. I was oblivious to their body language. I was unaware of their facial expressions. I would disregard their opinions if they didn't match mine. Then I wondered why they didn't contact me again. Why wasn't I invited to any gatherings? It left me feeling even more rejected and abandoned.

I would often come across as strong and intimidating. As if I knew it all. My demeanor was a double-edged sword. On one hand, I wanted to come across as confident. On the other hand, I wanted to come across as "Don't fuck with me." I guess the combination resulted in my coming across as cocky and mean. I am sure people could see right through me. I was the only one who couldn't see what I was doing. As the saying goes, "It is the darkest under the flame."

I would do my utmost best to "woo" the person in our first meeting. I would talk about my sexual abuse at the very first meeting in hopes that they would see me as honest and "special" in my suffering. Doesn't everyone want to hang out with a special person? In my mind, if I were special, then people would want to be my friend. I felt special in my specialness.

I couldn't understand why they still did not want to be my friend even after sharing how special I was in my suffering. No matter what I did or what I said, they did not want to be my friend. I felt rejected when I couldn't "enlist" them to be my "friend" who would validate my specialness. Who would join me in my misery? This perpetuated the lifelong cycle of my not feeling seen or heard, hence the need for being special, which in turn made me want to be even more special. If I couldn't be special in my accomplishments, maybe I could be special in my suffering. I thought that if I could be special somehow, I would be lovable enough to be seen, to be heard. It's no coincidence that my nickname is "See-me."

This, ladies and gentlemen, is what is known as narcissism in our society. A person you will be told to run away from. A person who will ruin your life. A person who will damage you.

I continued to play pretend that I was special until my older daughter broke the spell on April 18th, 2021, at Denver International Airport. It was 9:00 p.m. We had just claimed our luggage. The trip to Costa Rica was very healing. I had pulled my usual shenanigans of making myself look good at the expense of my older daughter. This was a typical pattern for me. I bad-mouthed her to a fellow traveler.

I'm guessing she was sick and tired of my belittling her.

"We need to talk," she said as soon as we got our luggage, while we were standing in the middle of baggage claim. "I have been waiting to talk to you all day long," she went on. "I was guided to watch a video last night on narcissism. I had never been able to put my finger on what is wrong with you. This video made everything clear. I can see it clearly now. You are a narcissist," she said firmly.

"Now is not a good time," I said, somewhat embarrassed and trying to figure out a way to deflect. But she wouldn't have it.

"It's never a good time, Mom," she continued, determined to be heard. "You are always worried about your image," she said self-assuredly.

"No, I am not," I denied. "It is not a good time because look at where we are. We are standing in the middle of baggage claim," I said in a meek attempt to preserve some of my false dignity, and my brain was frantically searching for an excuse. "But we can sit on the side and talk," I continued, hoping she would say that we can go home and talk.

"Okay, let's sit over there," she said, pointing to the window.

We walked over to the big windows of the baggage claim and parked ourselves and our luggage there. Once we sat down on the cold tiled floor, she schooled me for two hours on what a narcissist I was. This was the first time I'd heard this, and it began to open my eyes to my narcissistic behavior, which I was able to transcend through consistent inner child work. In the moment, it was as if I were hearing it from a distance. Nothing she was saying made sense, yet I felt very uncomfortable and had no rebuttal. That's how I knew there was truth behind what she was saying, even though none of it was resonating with me.

It felt like I was underwater, and the things she was saying to me felt more like an echo. It's as if her voice were muffled. I was having a hard time hearing her. This makes sense to me now as to why that was, knowing that the narcissistic persona is created by multiple personalities. In my case there were eighteen.

I had been doing my inner child work for the past nine years and had prided myself on being self-aware. But what my daughter was saying was completely news to me and took me by surprise. I had been feeling stuck on my spiritual path again and didn't know how to get unstuck. This incident came in the wake of my saying, "I am willing to look at this point of stuck-ness." I said this, praying to Theo.

"You are not special. There is nothing special about you. Stop pretending to yourself that you are special. There are a lot of people in this world who are special, and you are not one of them. What quality do you have that makes you so special? Just because you do your inner work, it doesn't make you special. There is nothing special about you," she repeated.

I couldn't face the reality that there was nothing special about me. What would I have if I didn't have my specialness? The only thing I had felt special about myself was my suffering and in this moment, I lost that too.

My daughter's words penetrated this shell that was made of specialness and put a crack in it. Enough of a crack that I could hear her voice, as muffled as it was. Enough of a crack that I could give myself permission to begin to see how I was not all that special.

It was very painful for me to admit to myself that I was not special. It broke my heart to hear my daughter talk like that. It broke my spirit to know how abusive I had been in my desperate effort to be special. But I knew this was something I needed to look at if I was to have a relationship with my daughter, if I didn't want to die alone and miserable. If I was to have a healthy business. If I was to have healthy relationships moving forward.

While I was embarrassed, I also saw the Love that was delivered in those two hours. Finally, someone cared enough to look deeper to see me for who I was. Someone who had the inner strength to help me to see my wrongdoings and shortcomings. Someone who was brave enough to demand better from me. There is no greater act of Love that I witnessed in my time here on earth.

My specialness was the water that I swam in. My specialness was the nourishment for my decaying self-esteem. My specialness gave me a purpose to live. It allowed me to have some dignity. My specialness gave me hope that someday I, too, would be loved. My specialness breathed life into me. Most of all, it was my air until I healed my mental illness. It was my friend when I was alone in the dark caverns of my traumas.

Outright abuse of a child breeds narcissism. Adults with avoidant attachment style tend to emotionally cut off relationships. Just as I did. These people are ultra-independent and have a hard time asking for help because the pain of rejection is too great. These people don't feel good enough and will often give of themselves to a fault to prove their worthiness. This makes us prey for those who take advantage of people like us.

My husband was a shopaholic. He figured I made enough money that he could visit India two or three times per year, sometimes leaving me with our two daughters while I was working two jobs to support his spending addiction.

He figured he could use me since I wasn't courageous enough to stand up for myself. He saw how willing I was to give of myself, not just my money. He also knew how insecure I felt about myself. He used my weaknesses against me to take advantage of me, and I did nothing, until my breaking point, that is. These are both narcissistic traits. His traits were of an over narcissist, while mine were those of a covert narcissist. We were two sides of the same coin.

I was on the phone with the babysitter as I was driving home from my second job. I was going let her know that I was on my way to pick up my daughter when I looked at the dashboard and saw the low gas light. I didn't know how long the light had been on for. Judging by the gas meter I knew it had been a while. Within thirty seconds of my noticing the light, my car began to stall. I was so overworked and overwhelmed that I didn't even notice when the gas light had come on, all because I wanted to make sure that I wasn't rejected and to prove that I was good enough.

Even though I was struggling to hold everything together, my desire to please him was very strong, and it was reflected in my actions. I gave him the permission to travel while taking on the burden of two jobs and taking care of my two young daughters. I had a strong urge to make sure that everything was in perfect order. That everything was lined up, from getting kids ready for school to making sure they were on time for their extracurricular activities, to the laundry being done on time, to making sure that the kids went to bed on time. While juggling their homework, arranging for a babysitter and my work and call schedules, and doing other household chores. I didn't want my husband to think I was a slacker. Nor did I want to have to ask him to do anything for me. After all, I was an independent woman. I was the maverick who could juggle it all without batting an eye. At least that is how I wanted to present myself to him. I did not want to him to see me as weak. The belief that I held was that those who are weak will be taken advantage of. Ironically, I was the victim of the very thing I was afraid of.

On the other hand, the urge to divorce him was just as strong. Nothing felt right about being with him. I just wanted to be done. It felt like it was too much. The conundrum was that my desire to be with him was just as strong as my desire to leave him. I didn't know which one I should follow as they were both compelling. I believe I was so afraid of being alone and that fear was blocking my clarity. Also, getting a divorce would mean that I somehow failed as a person. That I couldn't "keep it together." I was stuck in the moment between do I leave? Do I not leave?

This is the mind space of someone with disorganized attachment style. This leads us into discussion of how disorganized attachment style is formed and its symptoms in an adult.

Disorganized attachment style: This is a combination of both the anxious and avoidant attachments. It is the most complicated one out of the three. In this style, the child experiences inconsistency and abuse at the hands of the caregiver. On the one hand, he or she wants to be loved and cared for; on the other hand, they try to avoid the caregiver. There is this push and pull within the child. One part of the child is needy and wants to be clingy. The other part is avoidant. The child spends their adult life with this war of this push and pull on the inside.

As adults these people have difficulty forming relationships. When they do form a relationship, they tend to smother their partner in their effort to connect with them. Then when the partner inadvertently does something to hurt them, they cut their partner off completely. I personally feel this leads to the narcissistic cycle of love bombing someone when they first meet them, followed by the discard phase.

Early childhood trauma damages the psyche irreversibly. It inflicts deep injury on the brain. The effects of emotional injury to the brain are the same as physical injury. It affects both the structure and the function of the brain. The changes depend on the stage during which the trauma occurs and involve neurochemical changes, such as chronic secretion of cortisol and norepinephrine.

While we cannot heal the psyche, we can transcend it and think with our hearts. The mind is supposed to be the servant anyway. So why not support your heart back to health so that it can rule like the king that it is? The conundrum is that thinking with the heart is not possible until you have mended your broken heart. Inner child work can mend your broken heart. Therein lies your journey.

To mend your heart, you will have to nurse it back to health. You will have to hear its cries and feel its pain. You will have to listen to its call for help.

To nurture your heart back to its kingly state will require your dedication, consistency, commitment, and perseverance. It will require you to make it a way of life. Your inner children are formed when your heart gets broken. Your inner children carry the sorrow, the grief, and the pain of the trauma. When you get in touch with your inner child, you will know the pain that exists in your heart. Don't ignore your inner child. It is the portal to your heart. The inner child will shine the light onto your heart so you can assess the "damage." Are you ready to connect with your inner child?

This journey will require you to not give up on yourself. When you begin to connect with your inner child, you will encounter many challenges. I say this not to deter you from this work but rather to mentally and emotionally prepare you for it. Knowing what to expect as you progress on this journey is half the battle. One of those challenges will be your attachment wound(s). How you are attached to your caregiver will be reflected in your dealings with your inner child. Understanding different attachment styles will help you to overcome these challenges with cognizance and compassion so that you can begin to have a healthy relationship with yourself. So you can form a secure attachment with yourself. This in turn will help you to have a better relationship with others. Ultimately, it is all about you!

Chapter 7

Doing the Work

*A*s you just witnessed with my journey, the inner child work is a beautiful process imbued with depth and wisdom paving the roadway to self-realizations by the way of self-love. The journey will demand your very being. It will ask you to relinquish every part of *you* that you think is *you*. It will help you to skin the ego off your soul. It will debride your wounds to the core. Should you dare to embark on this journey, it will enlighten you.

Through sharing my journey with it, it is my intention to bring its spirit to life. It is my intention to give its spirit a Voice. I have heard many people flippantly say, "Oh, inner child work? I've been there, done that." After doing this work for twelve years I can tell you it's ever-evolving, and there is no "there." It's a dynamic process, and you are never done. There will always be another stalagmite and stalactite in the deep caverns of the mind waiting to be un-mined.

The benefits of this work are innumerable and boundless. Done with the right intention, this work will help you improve your finances, it will help you to have healthier relationships, and it will help you to enjoy physical health, on the surface. At a deeper level there are benefits for humanity that you may not be able to comprehend. The ripple effect of this work will extend out and touch humanity in ways that you cannot fathom. You are the creator of the universe and galaxies. But you have to take the time to cultivate the teachings that lie within this process. It is here to teach you if you care to learn.

While everyone can learn to do this work, it doesn't come without challenges. This book is being written with the intention to teach you the basics while giving you the understanding of the depths that it will take you to if you allow it. As you saw with my journey, it will take you along the different paths and bring you full circle back home to yourself. The journey will begin with you and end with you.

This work becomes much easier with knowledge and support. It is my intention to build a virtual support community via Facebook and eventually a physical support community that will become a way of life. For starters, each time the course is offered new students will be added to our community on FB. That way we can keep building our virtual village, which, it is my hope, will translate into physical villages down the road that will have a foundation of self-Love. A community cannot be built, nor can it thrive, without the foundation of self-Love.

You just witnessed the complexity of inner child work. Because we are multidimensional beings, so are our fragments. We have a mind, so do the fragments. Which means that every time the soul fragments, so does the mind. The mind is not equivalent to the brain. The mind is an abstract concept. The mind was originally designed to simply be the vessel that transfers information from the divine sea of consciousness to the brain. We all have one mind. Which means you and I think the same way and our traumas affect us the same way. This also means that the thoughts that you think also affect others. Consciousness is defined as "state of being aware." The more awake you are, the more aware you become.

When the sick mind begins to run your life, it makes it hard for you to do the inner child work. It will take you off on tangents. It will rationalize as to why you shouldn't do the work, or it will keep you busy so that you don't have the time to sit down and do your inner work. It does that because the trauma that caused the mind to split led to the belief that it is not good enough, that it is not worthy enough. So, the mind reasons that by looking at this issue of self-worth that you will prove to it that in fact you are not good enough or worthy enough.

The split mind is a fearful mind. It will use every trick in the book to try and distract you. This aspect makes inner child work extremely challenging, not to mention all the phases of growth it needs to go through for you to be able to integrate this part of you. It is doubly difficult to tune into all the aspects of the inner child, especially if you are new to this work. Hence the inspiration to write this book. This book was born out of the need for support while doing this crucial inner work, because as you heal your mind you are not just healing your mind itself, but rather healing the fragments of a fragmented mind. As we each do our part, we can eventually heal the deeply fragmented mind. Once the fragmented mind heals, we will have peace on earth.

Half the battle is mental preparation for this work. Please understand, you must be mentally prepared for this work. This work will awaken you. Sometimes the realizations will hit you like a ton of bricks, as if something just woke you up from deep sleep. It is not comfortable when someone turns on the lights while you are in deep sleep. As a result of your awakening, your relationships will change. Whatever is not in your best interest will leave you. Whatever does not resonate with your vibration as you evolve will dissolve. Be prepared for a different life than you are currently living. Once you awaken there is no turning back.

As you probably already guessed, the basis of inner child work is trauma. It is mostly associated with childhood trauma. But you can also have an adult child and a child from a past life, meaning if you experience trauma as an adult that part of you will fragment. The term child implies any part of you that is younger than you, which means you can have an adult inner child. First let's take a moment and define what trauma is. Trauma is anything that you perceive to be wounding, shocking, or distressing for you. Trauma does not always have to be a big event. It can be as little as, say, you came home late from school because you started playing with your friends and lost track of time, and when you got home your mom yelled at you. If you perceive that as trauma, then that was traumatic for you. Because we are all shaped differently because of our conditioning, what triggers one person may not trigger another.

The younger the age at which we experience trauma, the more damage it causes to our brain. There is a very thin tissue that connects our right hemisphere of the brain to the left hemisphere. This part is called the corpus callosum. The corpus callosum helps the two hemispheres of the brain to talk to each other. While the corpus callosum starts to develop at twenty weeks of gestation, it continues to thicken as the child grows up. The corpus callosum is responsible for integration of information, which helps us with perception. Research has shown a decrease in the thickness of corpus callosum in patients who experienced childhood trauma. Of course, childhood trauma also affects the brain in many other ways.

The moment you experience trauma, part of your soul fragments. This fragmented part of you stays stuck in that one moment of time and space in which the trauma occurred. That part of you keeps reliving that traumatic moment over and over by thinking about it again and again. This is what is known as post-traumatic stress disorder (PTSD). It's what I call "looping." You keep thinking the same thoughts over and over and can't seem to get them out of your head. The looping thoughts are formed by the neurons that are in the path of these thoughts. The imprint of these thoughts gets etched in the brain similar to ski tracks that are used over and over until they leave an imprint in the snow. In the same manner, when we think thoughts over and over, they leave an imprint in our brain, which means the older you get, the more solidified these tracks become. The more solid these tracks are, the harder it becomes to erase these tracks, making it harder to heal the psyche. The harder it becomes to heal the psyche, the more important it becomes to think with your heart rather than your mind. The more people that are looping, the more defects are caused in the collective psyche, the harder it has become to heal the psyche at a personal level.

To understand how trauma affects us, it is important to talk about the chakras. The word chakra comes from Sanskrit and means "wheel" or "circle." There are seven chakras associated with the physical body. These chakras are located on the glands and help the glands to function. Our science still doesn't know how the glands secrete the hormones that they do. When you awaken to who you are, you won't need science to explain to you what the chakras do. You will feel the energy, and you will simply know.

In the meantime, the chakras are vacuums that extract energy from the source and supply your organs with this God-like energy. This God-like energy is fuel for our body. It's what drives the body. It's what keeps us healthy. This energy is distributed to the organs by the way of a subtle energy system called the meridian or the nadis. It's the circulatory system for this God-like energy to be distributed to all of our trillions of cells. This is how the cells know how to undergo meiosis and mitosis and perform other cell functions. When the flow of this energy stops, we die. When the flow of this energy is blocked, we get ill.

When chakras are spinning at their optimal vibration, they help the energy to flow through the nadis (Sanskrit word meaning river) to provide sustenance to the tissue and the organs. This flow is reflected in their radiance. Karma is stored in the chakras and slows down their vibration and diminishes their radiance. The more Karma you accumulate, the lower the vibration of the chakras and the sicker you will become. The lower vibrating chakras are not able to extract divine energy from the ethers like they should. This means less fuel to the cells that are depending on the God-like energy to perform at their peak level.

The less blockage there is in the chakras, the more energy can flow through the nadis, providing sustenance to our tissues and organs. The purer the chakra is, the higher it vibrates and the greater its radiancy. Karma that we create from lifetime to lifetime gets stored in the chakras, unless you make a conscious effort to clear it. If you accumulate a lot of Karma, it slows down the vibration and radiancy of a chakra. Inner child work will help you to clear Karma from the chakras in a balanced way so they can begin to pull the divine energy from the ethers again. Over the years I have witnessed instantaneous healing many times clearing Karma using this method.

To help us to understand how this all works, Dr. Alberto Villoldo has also done much research on the chakras. He describes our chakras as funnel-shaped. The open end of the funnel sits about two to three centimeters outside of our physical body. The tip of the chakras one through five are attached to the spinal cord. When you experience trauma, the imprint of that trauma gets stored in your energy field electronically. When you encounter that same frequency of energy outside of you, that energy spills into the chakra system and hijacks your central nervous system. It's similar to turning on the light switch. You cannot stop the lights from going on once you hit the switch. Once the lights are on, you can turn them off, but there is nothing you can do in the middle to stop the lights from coming on. The same thing happens when we encounter energy that has the same electrical frequency as the energy of trauma that you experienced in the past. The energy spills into your chakras, which are attached to your spinal cord, and hijacks our central nervous system. From that point on, you are bound to your reaction. Your reaction is going to occur, and in that moment, there is nothing you can do to stop it. This is why Jesus said, "Forgive them, for they know not what they do."

In your moment of reaction, you are creating Karma. Just because you are not aware of what you are doing doesn't mean you are absolved from the consequences of your actions. The Law of Karma states that as you become an adult you have the responsibility to heal your trauma so that you don't go around hurting others. It offers no excuses. The Law of Karma encourages you to do your inner work so these reactions don't happen to begin with.

It also asks you to be proactive about clearing your Karma. You should not wait for an emotional reaction to happen because you cause a lot of trauma to others when you allow those reactions to occur, which in turn perpetuates the karmic cycle. As humans, you have been given the resources and the tools to take responsibility for your actions. Not everyone has these means to extricate themselves from their karmic predicament. This human life is an honor and a privilege. It is not granted to everyone.

While you cannot stop the reaction as it is happening, you can prevent the reaction from occurring by doing the inner child work. This is our duty as inhabitants of the earth. It is our emotions that create the universe. It is our emotions that determine whether there will be a tsunami. As within, so without applies 100 percent of the time. There are no exceptions to this rule. Let's first take care of the tsunami within so we can take care of the tsunami without. We are quick to blame things outside of us for our uncomfortability when all we need to do is go within. In the ancient times, when people saw a rise in the tide they would turn within and soothe their ruffled emotions because they knew that the high tide was simply a symptom of their inner turmoil. When they soothed their emotions, they noticed that the high tide would subside. They didn't have tsunamis back in the day because these ancient civilizations were in tune with their emotions.

This process will help your inner child to feel safe so there is no emotional chaos within you. You will become emotionally mature and stable, which will put the adult you in charge of your reactions. This does not mean that you will walk around being nice all the time. In fact, you will be whole in your day-to-day interactions. You will be able to tune into which emotion is appropriate to express at any given moment. You won't walk around smiling all the time or being angry all the time. You will be able to express your emotions, whether it's joy or anger, without getting lost in them. You will be able to express a wide octave of emotions without becoming them. You will take charge of your emotions rather than letting your emotions control you. The expression of your emotions will be from a place of Love rather than fear.

My parents had their own twisted way of thinking; they were proud Sikhs. Sikhs are not allowed to cut their hair. My mom used to tell this story as a way of conveying her family's devotion to their religion. Growing up in India, my mom was the oldest of the seven brothers and sisters. One day her youngest brother suffered a head injury and needed to be taken to the doctor. Once they arrived at the hospital the doctor asked her father if they could shave an area of the head so they could work around the wound that my uncle had incurred. "Dad said, 'Let him die,'" my mom says proudly. They attributed rigidity to devotion.

I am not sure what types of trauma my mom was dealing with at the time I was born, or how old the inner child was who was affecting her and her world view. I do know that she was not capable of being the mature adult that she needed to be to bear and raise two children. She would get upset and start yelling every thirty seconds, or so it seemed to little Simi.

I can hardly blame her as I was no different. I was in the body of a twenty-two-year-old with the mind of a six-month-old when I started to secretly date my boyfriend. I knew my parents would have to find out some day. I was happy to push off that day for as long as possible.

One day, the dreaded day came. We were at the beach in Milwaukee when someone from the congregation saw us. That man called my brother and told him that he saw us together. I was at home the following day when my brother approached me and asked me if I was with "Bhai Sahib." When I heard the words, as if through a tunnel, I felt the floor move from underneath my feet. My gut twisted in a tight knot. My heart started to beat fast. My feet felt glued to the ground along with my eyes. I could not look him in the eyes and said, "Yes," which was barely audible.

He said, "If you don't tell Mom and Dad, I will. So let me know what you wanna do. Are you going to tell them, or should I?"

"I will," I said meekly, while trying not to show the horror that I was feeling, still looking down. I wouldn't dare look him in the eyes.

"Well, you need to tell them by Sunday, if you don't, I will," he said again with a firmness in his voice. He seemed serious, and I didn't think I could talk him out of it. I knew the time had come to let my parents know that I had been dating our married Sikh priest for the past year.

I had to come clean. I knew that it wouldn't go over well. I had no choice but to divulge the truth. By then, I had become a pathological liar. This was the only situation that they knew I had lied about. My whole life had become one big lie. This was not the only situation I had lied about. I was someone else at home and a completely different person outside. As if I led a double life.

The migration to the states birthed another version of Simi. A version that escaped my parents' view until the day I eloped with my boyfriend. I was in fifth grade, and we had to swim as part of the phys ed. I had my pigtails, my one-piece swimsuit, and a veil of hair covering my legs and my crotch, which my mother would braid if she had her way. We are hairy people.

We are born that way. If it was a medical condition, at least I would have an excuse. But no such luck. As I stepped out into the pool area, I saw all heads turn toward me, staring at me as if they had seen a UFO, all with dumbfounded looks. Mouths hanging open was the welcome I received on my very first visit to the pool. I could hear the echo of their snickering as I walked toward the water.

I was not going to go to school like that again. I knew that my mother, being the devout Sikh she was, would rather I be ridiculed than allow me to shave my legs. After all, her father was okay with her brother dying. I could certainly be humiliated. I also knew she wanted to follow in her father's footsteps. I figured if I couldn't shave my legs, I could certainly Nair them. I decided it was better to ask for forgiveness than permission. I guess my mother had a lot to forgive as I grew older. But what I didn't know was that my mother would have a lot to forgive all at once!

Deceit and disingenuity soon became a way of life for me. I did what I needed to do to not be buried by opprobrium and infamy while living in the land of the free. Little Simi got lost in the differences between the east and the west. She was drowning between Sikhism and Christianity. Everything around her threatened to demolish and abolish her sense of self. Pleasing the parents at home. Appeasing the peers at school.

Once my parents found out they tried to maintain their calm, but I could feel the ticking of the bomb underneath their calm demeanor. They started talking about taking me to India to get me married. That was my biggest nightmare. I knew that after living in America I couldn't be a submissive housewife to an Indian family. I was also afraid that the family would somehow find out about my sexual abuse and would judge me for not being a virgin. There were so many thoughts going through my head that I couldn't take it anymore. I couldn't think about the what-if scenarios. What if they found out that I was sexually abused? What if they found out that I was not a virgin? What if they found out I was messed up? What if they wanted me to stay at home and cook and clean?

The weight of all the lies and pretenses felt heavy on my young shoulders. The easiest thing to do would be to elope with my boyfriend. At least all the lies would stop. At least I wouldn't need to live two lives. We had known that my parents would never accept this relationship. So, we had saved up a few thousand dollars in case we needed to elope.

My parents didn't want to let me out of their sight. They also didn't want me to rebel. A couple days after the whole blow-up I told them I needed to go to the library. I took some clothes with me, got in my car and left home, never to return.

I saw nothing wrong with what I was doing. Remember I was in my early twenties with the mind of an infant. I felt so invisible that I didn't think that my parents would even notice that I was gone. It wasn't until I was forty-three years old and had been doing my spiritual work that I realized the enormity of my actions; the devastating pain I caused my parents. The disgrace they experienced at the hands of the Indian community was simply horrifying. There was an onslaught of insults from people who took the liberty to call them to tell them what a slut I was. Someone called and said, "If it was my daughter, I would have pulled the trigger on her." One idiot even flew to California because he thought my boyfriend and I had gone there. The joke is on him because we were in Atlanta, Georgia.

Plenty of sadistic spectators took pleasure in witnessing the slaughtering of a family, a heritage. Blind to the tears of butchered hearts. Wrapped up in their uncouthness, unwilling and incapable of facing the truth that I was the product of the conditioning of a culture and religion to which they also contributed. Everyone was busy casting stones as if they were unblemished. As if they were flawless. I was the scapegoat of my ancestral lineage, bearing the burden of their wrongdoings. I was simply the culmination of the cascading domino effect that started possibly thousands of years ago. I became the maelstrom to sweep away the remnants of a foundation that consisted of the bones of virtues upheld by a thread, causing devastating destruction in my wake. Or so it appeared.

The price of dismantling this foundation was steep. I became odious overnight. I was exiled from the community and ostracized from the family. No one wanted their sons or daughters to hang out with a homewrecker. No one wanted to be seen with a harlot. No one wanted to be associated with a Jezebel. I stopped being invited to gatherings, birthdays, and weddings. I wasn't even told about the funerals either as if I had leprosy. My sentence? Banishment from community for life without trial or parole.

Inner child work will help you to end the cycle of trauma. The buck stops with you. It does not have to infiltrate your future generations. Your process will be completely different from mine. Allow the process to take you where it needs to take you so that you can heal at your core.

As you begin the process you will begin to experience a series of grief reactions followed by a series of softening. Grief is how we cope with loss. Most often it is a topic of discussion when there is some sort of a loss in life. Loss of a loved one or divorce are a couple of examples of when someone might grieve.

On this journey, you will experience perceived loss of what could have been. You will see what your life would have been like if you had not experienced trauma. You will see how trauma has shaped your life. When you compare your life and what could have been to what it is, you will mourn the loss of a life that could have been. It is important to move through all stages of grief so you can heal.

There are several stages of grief as defined by the Swiss psychologist Elizabeth Kubler Ross, who wrote on death and dying:

1. Denial

2. Anger

3. Bargaining

4. Depression

5. Acceptance

The stages are similar in the process of enlightenment. There are six stages in awakening:

1. Denial

2. Bargaining

3. Anger

4. Sadness

5. Acceptance

6. Self-Love

We are all in denial. We are a bunch of liars. We lie to ourselves all the time. We often pretend to be somewhere we are not. We pretend as if everything is okay. It is hard for us to admit to ourselves that we are not *feeling* okay, that there is something off. Once we realize we are in denial we go into doubt. We begin to question if indeed we are in denial. This is why Jesus said, "Don't undo in doubt what you did in faith." Then we go through anger and sadness. These may change from moment to moment. One minute we may feel angry, the next minute we may feel sad. Our job is to ride the tide of emotions. This may last from days, to weeks, to months, to perhaps even years depending on the depth of the trauma.

If you can simply be present with your emotions, you will automatically come to a place of acceptance. Self-Love comes after acceptance and is truly Divine Grace. You can't consciously try to love yourself. It will happen to you rather than your reaching for it. When you feel love for yourself you will notice that you are not judging others. When you love yourself, you cannot dislike or hate another. It is important to be aware of these stages so you can work through your trauma and have a sense of what is happening. This will help to empower you.

Chapter 8

Let the Preparations Begin

*L*IKE ANY GRAND JOURNEY, PREPARATION for this work is not just required but is essential because it sets a foundation upon which you will build your life of freedom. The stronger the foundation, the bigger the life you can build upon it. This includes physical, emotional, and mental preparation. A solid foundation is set when all of the components are aligned for a smooth journey.

Mental

Along with physical and emotional preparation, mental preparation is just as important. You will need to let go of certain thought patterns that hold you back. This journey will require you to give up who you are to become who you want to be.

This is a process of awakening. When you are ready things will be revealed to you and not a moment sooner. They will hit you like a ton of bricks. As I've said, with this process you are awakening your mind that is asleep. It is akin to turning on the bright lights when someone is in a deep sleep. When you turn on the bright lights when someone is asleep, you shock them into awakening. Don't be surprised at the revelations you may experience as you begin this work. It is your job to follow through with the inspired action steps and not negate the inspiration you will receive. It is your journey and yours alone. No one can walk it for you. Expect your life to change, especially if you are willing to do your inner work and then follow through with the inspired action step(s). The process unfolds as you do your inner work, which then culminates in an inspiration to take a physical action step. If you don't take that action step you will not be able to move forward in your journey until you do. It's like a math class. You cannot learn your multiplication tables until you learn addition. Each step is built on the last, and discernment is needed.

Part of the mental preparation is setting intentions. Let's delve into the art of setting intentions that will splash your life with the colors of joy, abundance, and peace.

When you set your intentions, your conscious mind is letting your subconscious and unconscious mind know what you want to do, because it's your subconscious and your unconscious mind that help you to manifest. To recruit them you have to let them know what you want to do so they can prepare to help you. Be discerning when you set your intentions. Little intentions will deliver small results, and before you know it you will be setting intentions again. You will not be able to propel your life forward with momentum like you want to if you become afraid to set big intentions. Don't be woeful. Be bold so your life can be bold.

Setting Intentions

Intentions are your inner GPS. Setting your intentions is like entering a destination in your GPS. It tells the universe where you want to go. Without intentions, it is like getting in the car being ready to drive but not knowing where it is that you are going. Without knowing where you are going you won't get anywhere. Intentions are important for manifesting the life of your dreams. Word your intentions in a positive manner and go as big as you can. This is your time to ask the universe for what you want. As they say, ask and it is given. So, ask for something so big that you don't have to ask again. If you do ask for something big, yes, it might take you longer to get there, but once you get to your destination, you will be satisfied.

Your intentions are your heart's desires. Your intentions are what your heart wants you to have. The heart gets what the heart wants because the heart is the king! The way to manifest anything is to drop into your heart. Tap into your heart's desires. Use discernment that it is not the mind that is acting as the impersonator of the heart. The mind is tricky and will trick you into thinking that it's the heart when in reality it's the mind.

For you to listen to your heart, you will need time. Don't try to rush this process, as this process cannot be rushed. We have ignored the Voice of the heart for so long that it will take time to tune into it and discern it. As you take the time to listen to it, it will become louder over time.

As you begin to set your intentions, set aside an evening so you can listen deeply, so you don't feel hurried. At first the mind will speak loudly to get your attention. Allow this voice of the mind to get as loud as it wants to. Simply be present to all that the mind wants. Then, as you sit there, observing, you will begin to hear a small Voice, a Voice that is not so loud, a Voice that is not commanding your attention. This Voice is gentle and clear without the baggage of emotion. Listen for that small Voice. That small Voice is your heart. What does it have to say? Does it inspire you? Is it compelling even though it's soft? Allow this Voice to take center stage. Give it the time and attention that it deserves. Write down what the Voice wants. Let this be your guidepost. It is no different than meditation. I simply sat there watching my breath and allowed the thoughts to arise from within me. I sat there in stillness until I got clarity that I had received my intentions from the heart.

You will notice that once you have set your intentions, seemingly irrelevant events, circumstances, and situations will appear. Your job is to discern what the Voice is guiding you to do. You will need to slow down and take the time to listen, to discern what you are being called to do. Follow the Voice. It is your heart guiding you to your health, your healing. The mind will fight you. It will get louder. The more you tune into the Voice, the louder the mind will get, the more assertive it will become. Your job is to keep following the Voice no matter what the mind says.

This is where things get a little tricky. Remember that when we experience trauma the mind splits. It splits into the lower and the higher mind. The higher mind is calm and nonreactive. It is patient and waits for the instruction from the heart before acting. Unfortunately, because of the split the lower mind gets in the way by talking louder and getting angry. The lower mind is your inner saboteur. The lower mind is highly reactive. It gets triggered at the drop of a hat. Both of the minds are extremely powerful. It's with the help of the mind that the heart is able to manifest its desires. They work hand-in-hand. To manifest something of substance that is not chaotic, the mind needs to follow the heart's lead. When the mind is split, only the higher mind is able to follow the heart's lead. This leaves the lower mind free to do and create what it wants to do and create. This makes the lower mind unpredictable. Inner child work helps to integrate the lower with the higher mind so that it is not so reactive.

The unpredictability of the lower mind is what makes it dangerous. The challenge is that the lower mind is both stupid and powerful. Not a good combination to have. The idea is to navigate around the lower mind with precision. The kind of precision that you and I can't navigate with our conscious mind. We need higher help. I don't know about you, but I wouldn't make one single move without first confirming that was what was required of me.

Discernment is an art. Like any other muscle, it takes practice to build it. The way to strengthen a muscle is through practice. The word practice means to apply a skill repeatedly until you get better at it. Which means there will be times when you will make a mistake. Your inner guide will help you to bring awareness to whether or not you listened to the Voice. Trust this process. This is how you will learn to differentiate between the Voice of the heart and the voice of the ego. The Voice of the heart is not very loud. It is softer. It comes through with purity and clarity. When I hear the Voice, I know it to be true in my heart. Because it feels like it is arising from somewhere deep within me. If I had to pinpoint the area, I would say it feels like it is arising from where my physical heart is. The Voice tells me that it arises from my Sacred Heart, which is the space that lies directly outside of my physical heart. When the Voice is speaking, I have no doubts and my heart feels open. There is no tightness in my chest. The deeper you go into this journey, the harder the lessons will be, just as the crucifixion was a big lesson for Jesus, part of his destiny and his service to humanity all in one. That's when discernment is needed the most. It is best to start exercising this muscle early on. So, you get better at it by the time you get to your moment of "crucifixion," because we all have one for such is the process. This is not always physical. This could be emotional. It is something you give up in service to humanity. I will say that the higher your calling is, the harder your lessons will be. Just like if you wanted to become a mathematician, you will have to take higher levels of math than if you wanted to study medicine. It is part of the training to prepare you for your higher calling.

The lower mind literally has the power to kill you, especially if you try to awaken too quickly. The lower mind is highly reactive. When you awaken, you are awakening to how reactive the lower mind is. Your lower mind is the ego, and ego does not want to die. By definition, awakening is the death of the ego. If you try to let the ego go too quickly it will kill you. This is why you can't rush the process. This is why discernment is important. This is why it's important to tune into the Voice. The Voice is all-knowing and will guide you with precision.

For instance, I was stuck in my psyche with my narcissism. I did not know how to extricate myself out of my mental illness and felt helpless. Of course, my older daughter knew that was my struggle and had several dreams that my mental illness was way bigger than me. When she would have those dreams, she would tell me to take psilocybin. I would turn within to ask the Voice if I was supposed to take psilocybin and each time, I heard a "no" and felt a tightness in my chest reflecting that answer as well. I was extremely frustrated because little Simi wanted to get to the end zone as quickly as possible. But I knew I needed to follow guidance if I was to make it out of my mental prison. The Voice guided me to continue to strengthen my heart by doing the inner child work. This would frustrate my daughter to no end.

Then one day in February of 2023, my older daughter mentioned mushrooms again, once again I tuned into the Voice and this time, I received a green light to go ahead and start. I felt the chest tightness go away, reflecting a "yes." The Voice taught me how to work with mushrooms in a way so that I could attain enlightenment. I realized after the fact that we get enlightened when the heart is strong enough to take over the mind. If the heart is not strong enough to take over the mind, then the mind can attack the heart and kill you because it will feel threatened. It is truly a battle between the heart and the mind until the time of enlightenment. Of course, it's a little more complicated than that, but this gives you a glimpse of how important it is to follow the Voice when on this path.

I was tuned into the Voice like the note into the key. The Voice was my savior. Your Voice will serve as yours. It will help you to navigate so that you trigger the mind just enough but not so much that it will lead you to your demise. Be ready to get out of your comfort zone. Be ready to feel uncomfortable. Be ready for your Masterhood.

This is not easy to navigate if you do it by yourself. This is why you need the Voice of the heart. Only the king within you knows how to help you. There is an army of spirit guides, of which your Higher Self is the captain. Together they will help you reach the next milestone. You have to follow the Voice with precision and skill, which means your full dedication to this work is required. You can't half-ass it.

This journey will lead you to your Masterhood. Being a Master is no joke; it is a serious business. You have the power within you to create universes. For you to do that you have to be well-trained. Listening to the Voice is part of that training. Are you ready to step into the Mastery School that is within you?

Back to Basics

The way to tune into your intentions is by bringing awareness to your emotional storage shed (ESS). This is the area in the middle of your upper chest, in between the throat and the heart chakra. You will notice some feelings and desires that want to express themselves through you. Tune into that area for as long as you need to. Keep your focus on the area on your chest as you breathe in and out. Don't alter your breath, just watch it come in and go out. Eventually you will get in thought forms about what your heart's desires are. Make sure to have paper and pen ready. Your heart thinks via feelings. When these feelings get translated to thoughts you will know what your heart's desires are. To allow this process to unfold you have to allow time, awareness, and space for this process to emerge from you. If you give it enough attention for a long enough time, the thoughts from the heart will arise to reveal themselves to you. All that is required is your presence. You will simply know that the intentions are coming from the heart because they will feel pure, genuine, and supportive. It took me about two or more hours the first time I sat down to grab those intentions.

You will have doubts as to whether or not you can do this. And that is okay. Allow the doubts to arise, but don't let them hold you back. It is okay to feel frustrated or even annoyed when you, at first, don't get clear answers. Don't let that deter you. Acknowledge the feelings and keep observing. Don't let the lies of your mind hold you back from seeking out the life you want to live.

Intentions are magical and pave the road for miracles to happen in your life. Once you set an intention, the universe begins to conspire on your behalf. Now the universe knows what you want, and it does its utmost best to deliver it to you. If there are blocks on your path the universe will reveal those blocks to you so you can clear them. This revelation of blocks is not a punishment but rather an act of Love by the universe, because if you don't know about the blocks you can't clear them. The universe even supports you in clearing those blocks. It will show you ways to clear them. It will inspire you to take action to clear your path. Remember the path is yours to walk. The universe can simply point the way, because you are God in drag, and the universe cannot supersede your free will. Some of the roadblocks will be harder to clear than others. Your willingness to clear these blocks is what is required. This is why you can't half-ass this journey.

For instance, if you are being inspired to let go of a relationship that is hindering you and you choose not to, the Voice will continue to remind you of that same step over and over until you listen. If you don't listen or don't know to listen, you will remain stuck, and you will feel stuck in your life and on your path. For me, I was guided to leave my marriage of twenty years. Shortly after, I was guided to leave my job, a job that paid more than a quarter million dollars per year. I was told to downsize to prepare myself for what was to come because I was going on a journey.

As I continued to prepare for this mysterious expedition, I sold everything I owned. I gave up my luxury car. All of this happened over a period of fourteen months. My older daughter ran away from home shortly after she turned eighteen after enduring years of abuse. I left my younger daughter with her dad so that I could embark on this vagrant voyage. So that I could become the mother that I wanted to be. So that I could Love them instead of abuse them. This was my way of loving them so much that I was willing to change for them. My only companions on this journey were a small flame of intentions lighting the way, a touch of willingness to walk this path, and spikes of trust to keep my feet steady on the ever so icy grounds that I was being called to walk upon. These events began to transpire within a couple of years after I wrote down my intentions.

The intentions that emerged through me when I first sat down to write them are still unfolding almost fifteen years later. I will list a few of my intentions that emerged. I hope this helps you to reach for those deeper desires of your heart.

1. My intention was to be vigilant only for the kingdom of God—I wanted to be enlightened.

2. My intention was to see things differently—I wanted to shift my perception of the world.

3. My intention was to realize the God within.

4. My intention was to live a life full of abundance, joy, and peace.

5. My intention was to have healthy relationships, friendships, and partnerships.

6. My intention was to be a beacon of light for this world.

Physical Preparation

This part will also help you with mental preparation, as they are all intertwined. Begin by gathering the ingredients needed for this process. Grab a journal or a notebook. A pen. A candle, preferably without chemicals, and incense with an incense holder. Create a sacred space for yourself. By creating a physical space, you are grounding your intention to do this work into the physical realm. You are bringing the unmanifest into the manifest. It will solidify your intentions. In this case, your intention is to set a solid foundation. The physical space is preferably an altar. Altar doesn't necessarily have to be anything extravagant.

When I first started, I didn't have a private space for me that I could escape to. I put up curtains (with the help of my husband) around an empty space in the basement, next to the furnace. It was maybe five-by-five feet in dimension. This way I would have some privacy. Then I took a cardboard box and taped both ends shut. I draped the box with a small white tablecloth and placed figurines of Buddha and Jesus on it along with some tea candles and incense. I made it my own. I was neither a Buddhist nor a Christian; rather, I valued their teachings. I was inspired by them. I wanted to be like them. I didn't worry about what my husband was going to think or not think. I didn't worry about whether I was betraying my religion. The only force driving me was my sheer desire to heal. I had to go beyond the right and wrongdoings. I had to go beyond my own mind. I had to go beyond my teachings as a Sikh. I had to follow my heart. I had to tune into what I wanted. I had to listen to the Voice.

This was the first time in my life I didn't feel so lost. Even though nothing about my altar was related to Sikhism, I felt at home. I felt nurtured and nourished. From that moment on, I made it all about me. I couldn't wait until my kids were older. I couldn't wait for my husband to approve of what I was doing. I couldn't stand to betray myself a moment longer. I was going to begin the journey by hook or by crook. I was willing to lose everything to find myself. The Voice kept me going. It compelled me to take the steps I needed to take to materialize the kind of life my heart desired. It showed me the way to heal my heart. My only job was to listen.

I, the soul, was so determined in starting my journey that anyone who came in between me and my path was obliterated. My marriage was getting in my way, so I let it go. When I had to work to support the material things, including the house I had, they were let go. My job was taking up too much of my time, so it was let go. There even came a time when I felt my kids were in the way, so they too were let go. Then the town and state I lived in were getting in the way, so I moved to a different state where I knew no one, where I didn't have a job, a family, or friends to distract me. Little did I know I was being readied for a battle within myself. I want to clarify that it's not that I didn't Love my kids. How can I not Love them when they are a part of me both literally and figuratively? For we are all one. I knew that if I couldn't Love myself, then I couldn't Love anyone else. This was my journey into self-Love, and I had to claim it.

When I cleared these things out of the way, then came the hardest part. That part was the battle between the heart and the mind. It was an internal war. A Mahabharat. My body was the battlefield and my soul was the soldier. My soul had to choose who to side with at any given moment. The soul was the nurse to the heart and a slave to the mind. Who will I choose to serve?

The mind was unrelenting, no holds barred, telling me all kinds of lies. It told me I wasn't important enough. It told me I was worthless. It told me I wasn't pretty enough. It told me I wasn't skinny enough. It told me I wasn't rich enough. It told me I wasn't poor enough. It told me no matter what I did, I would never be enough. It told me I was worse than shit because the shit at least served a purpose to cleanse the body.

The mind was ruthless. It was cruel. It was callous. It was like an incessantly violent, untamed, rabid dog. Its assault was overwhelming and became unbearable a lot of the time. It would have been happy had I committed suicide. That's when I needed the tenacity to march forward. The strength and determination to not give up on myself. I needed hope to win this war. It took all I had. It took me to the pinnacle of darkness within me where I had no hope and didn't want to live. It was during these times that I knew my Higher Self was there to instill a drop of hope in me. She imbued me with courage to not listen to the lies of the mind. She held my hand and gently led me down the pathway that terrified me to show me that I have the power within me to continue to choose the Voice in spite of the mind.

My heart cried, hearing the onslaught of insults the mind was throwing at me, the soul. The heart was too weak. It didn't have the strength to stand up to the bully. It didn't have the courage to stand up to the tyrant who had taken over in the moment. I could feel the weakened and broken heart. It couldn't get up from its knees. The heart was not yet strong enough to take over the mind. But its was getting stronger by the moment. I could feel it. I could hear it loudly. I could feel the strength behind the Voice.

It was because of the inner child work.

The choice to go on this path had to come from the soul. It is ultimately the soul that chooses whether to serve the heart or be a slave to the mind. The choice to stop the chaos. The choice to stop the abuse. The soul in me had to say *enough!* It had to stand up for itself to stop the merciless attack. Something had to give, and it wasn't going to be me this time around.

For the next eight years, I mended my heart so it would become strong enough to take over the mind. That was the only way. The monkey mind needed a trooper. That trooper is the heart, and it fought for the heart. I mended my heart. I nursed it back to life with the help of my HS. It was all done through strengthening the Voice.

The day came when the Voice became so strong that it put the mind in its place. It reminded the mind that it is the slave and to know its place. It reminded the mind that it is the servant, not the master. It called out the mind's facade of being sorrowful over its deeds. It called out the mind for shedding crocodile tears for the way it's behaved. In crude language the mind was told to shut the fuck up by the same Voice that had begun ever so softly. The same Voice I had to work really, really hard to listen to. Yes, it was the same Voice.

During the months that followed, I was taught how to think with my heart. I was taught how to speak from the heart. I was taught how to act from the heart. I was taught that the heart can be just as crude as the mind in the name of justice and justice only. The heart will not stand by and be abused. The heart is not all airy-fairy. The heart is a chameleon. It will show kindness and compassion with firmness. It will express its softness through its Voice of steel. It demands and commands respect. It finds joy in others' happiness. It knows when to speak up and when to surrender. These are the skills of a true leader.

All this time the mind was the pretender, pretending to be the heart while mercilessly killing. The heart will also kill mercilessly when needed, but it will come from a place of love rather than fear. Look at the goddess Kali. She is a Hindu deity who is both the goddess of destruction and creation. Her name literally means darkness. She is the destroyer of evil. She liberates humanity from ego through destructive forces. You see it's all in your intention. On the surface the actions look the same but in reality, they are in fact quite different.

It's the Voice of the heart that matters. Who is the mind to judge? But it will judge until the heart gains enough strength to take over the mind. Until we have dropped into our heart, we have no right to judge. The judgment will prevail as in the Law of Karma. But only while operating from a place of Love and justice rather than fear and facade.

Don't place the heart in another box. Don't try to figure out what the heart wants with your mind. If you do, you will fail miserably. Hence the state of humanity. We have tried to figure out what the heart wants with the mind. The heart is no longer willing to stay quiet while the mind commits atrocious crimes against humanity. Thinking with your mind is no longer an option. Inner child work will pave the way for the Voice of the heart.

Be so steadfast on this journey that nothing and no one can get in the way. Give yourself permission to be you, just as I did, unconstrained by anything outside of you. This is a quiet kind of rebellion. The kind of rebellion that doesn't hurt anyone. The kind of rebellion that honors you while honoring others even though it may not seem like it on the surface. The kind of rebellion that demands your very best. The kind of rebellion that challenges you to step into your power. The kind of rebellion that empowers, not disempowers. Most of all, it's the kind of rebellion that is guided by your Higher Self. If it is the right kind of rebellion, it will bring peace to your heart, not another uprising. Rise above it all because *you* matter.

I began my journey by sitting in this small space, with walls made of thin, white curtains. Before beginning my practice for the day, I would light a candle in honor of me and my journey, along with an incense stick. The incense helped me to get present in the moment, The lighting of the candle symbolized the lighting of my spiritual path so I could see the way. Intention with discernment became my internal candle, my lamp that lit the way. Then I would sit in meditation for at least five minutes. I initially started out by setting a timer. This way I would make sure that I sat for at least five minutes. As I began to meditate regularly, I no longer needed a timer. Theo recommended meditation no less than five minutes and no more than thirty minutes per day. I followed their instructions to the T.

Shortly after I began my practice, my husband began to make fun of my space by calling it a "ghost mansion." I had grown accustomed to his psychological abuse. I did not have the courage to stand up to him. I had felt uncomfortable meditating in front of him because I knew he would make some backhanded comment or another. He was ridiculing me because he wanted me to stop. That was the reason why I had asked him to help me put up the curtains. It was my way of asking for permission in hopes that he wouldn't mock me. At that moment, I decided I was not going to allow him to know when I was meditating. I was not going to allow him to stop me.

The wheels in my mind began to turn. *When could I meditate so he wouldn't know?* This was very difficult because he was a stay-at-home dad and would make sure that he was at home when I came home from work. He liked to micromanage me and my time. But the Voice gave me a brilliant idea!

We knew another couple with whom we would get together quite frequently. Since my husband was a stay-at-home dad, he would usually schedule our evening gatherings and planned them around the time when I would get home from work, which left no time for me to meditate without him knowing about it. I also did not want to tell him to plan the gatherings around my meditation time because I did not want to be mocked or stopped.

One evening once we got to this couple's house I went into the bathroom and sat on the bathroom floor to meditate for twenty minutes or so. I would flush the toilet and wash my hands afterward to make it appear more real that I had used the bathroom. No, it was not an ideal place for meditation. It was not your picture-perfect scene. If I wasn't meditating in our friend's bathroom, I was doing meditation in our bathroom. This way I got some privacy, and no one had to know about my business and it got the job done. As they say, "Where there's a will, there's a way."

Indeed, where there was a will, a way opened up. You just have to be open to walking the way. It may not look like what you want it to look like. Never did I imagine meditating in a bathroom. When I saw pictures of someone meditating it was in a serene, clean, quiet place by the oceanfront or mountaintop somewhere. I have yet to see a picture of someone meditating along the toilet bowl and breathing in the microdroplets in the air while trying to quiet the mind. It was a true test, I would say.

Meditating in the bathroom taught me to quiet my mind regardless of my surroundings. It taught me that the place doesn't matter. What matters is that you do it. If it is truly your will to do this work, you will find a way. When you do, you will notice that events will take place in your life that will support you on your path.

I wanted to heal so badly that there was nothing and no one who was going to get in my way of meditating. I was so miserable in life and didn't know how to emerge from the mess that I had created. I had neither the courage nor the clarity to figure out how to get out of this abusive relationship that I had been in for the past twenty years! I trusted the Voice to guide me.

People often would ask me how I stay motivated to do this work. My response was, how are you *not* motivated to do this work? Because life is full of suffering. I can't comprehend why someone wouldn't want to extricate themselves from this suffering. When you heal yourself, you can live a life of abundance, joy, and freedom. Why wouldn't you choose to heal yourself?

Emotional

As I alluded to above, be willing to feel the uncomfortable emotions instead of shoving them down. When the mind is triggered, you will feel uncomfortable emotions. Be very present to that discomfort that your feelings produce. Lean into it instead of resisting it. Get to know the emotions. They are telling you something. They are telling you a story. A story of your heart. Are you willing to listen to the calling of your heart?

The challenge is that most of us are numb to our feelings. This part will take some practice. The more you practice the better you will get, just like with anything else. The mind will try to get in the way by telling you that you are doing it wrong. I can tell you that you can't do this wrong. When the mind talks like that it means you are on the right path. This is good news. No, it doesn't always feel the most comfortable, but nonetheless it is a guidepost that you are on your way. In fact, the greater the resistance, the greater the healing will be once you come out on the other side of it.

Feel your emotions in your upper chest between your throat and your heart chakra, in your emotional storage shed, your ESS. This is an important area because all your emotions, memories, and experiences are stored in this area. This is your access point that is sequential but not linear, nor is it practical. Your emotions lead you into different dimensions so you can experience the fullness of who you are. They are the gateway to any experience you may have experienced ever since your creation. They will guide you to the next layer that you need to peel off.

Trusting the process is an important part of the journey. Only those emotions will surface, those that need to be cleared to move on to the next set of emotions or story. They like to tell a story through feelings, which then gets translated into thoughts and then words. You may want to write the essence of these stories down.

Start your practice by bringing awareness to this area on your upper middle chest. You can touch the area gently and rub it in a circular manner to attune to it. What do you feel when you first touch this area? If you don't feel anything, that's okay. Throughout the day, touch this area and see what you feel. The more awareness you bring to this area, the more attuned you will become, and soon you will be able to feel emotions that reside in this area.

Touching this area is akin to inserting a key in a lock. Rubbing this area is akin to turning the key in the lock. If the lock happens to be a bit rusty you may need to try wiggling it a few times to get it to open, so don't give up. Your hand is the key to the lock of your emotional storage shed. The lock was placed there because you weren't ready to look at its content. You are ready now (otherwise you wouldn't be reading this book), and it is time to open that lock with eagerness, patience, gratitude, respect, and sacredness for what it holds, for it holds the key to your liberation.

Remember that it is a journey, and there is no destination. However, there are milestones along the way that confirm for us that the work that we are doing is not in vain.

Now that you are prepared to begin this journey go ahead; light a candle, burn that incense stick, grab a pen and paper, and get started! Happy odyssey!

Chapter 9

Jumpstart Your Healing Journey Now

MAKE SOME TIME IN YOUR day to sit in a meditative state. Have your pen and paper ready. Make sure there are no disturbances or distractions. As you sit, ask yourself: *What annoyed, frustrated, or angered me today?* After you have asked yourself this question, bring your awareness to your breath. Keep your focus on your breath while bringing your awareness to the ESS until you receive an answer. Don't go searching for it with your mind. The Voice will let you know what situation is coming forward. We are an onion; we have layers and layers of trauma stored in our soul. In fact, the energies of the trauma are compressed within our soul. Which makes it very difficult to reach the core. There is no way you can begin to figure out which layer needs to be peeled off next.

The Voice has the innate wisdom to know which situation will peel off the next layer of the onion. Trust the Voice to guide your path. Allow the answer to come to you. It may come to you in thought form or a vision. Have no expectations as to how it's going to come. Allow it to arise from within you. A situation will come to mind. If it doesn't, that means your mind is talking too much. Quiet the mind by spending extra time watching your breath go in and come out. Take as long as you need to. Again, don't rush this process because it will only slow you down.

Once you know what annoyed, frustrated, or angered you, then feel that emotion by bringing your attention to your emotional storage shed (ESS). Feel the essence of the emotions(s) that you felt in that particular situation. Figure out all of the emotions this situation brought up. When you tune in in this manner you will also begin to get familiar with the vibration and the energy of these emotions, which will help you discern which inner child it is as you begin to become whole. You likely have more than one inner child. Theo said that on average we have four to six inner children. I had eight, including past-life inner children. Once you have tapped into all of the emotions, ask yourself, "When was the first time I ever felt these particular emotions?" Again, wait for the answer to come and find you. You will notice that a circumstance from your childhood will come to mind. If it's not from your childhood, ask yourself to keep going back until you find an event that occurred in your childhood. Your inner children can have different personalities as well. In my case I had eighteen multiple personalities.

Whatever comes up, work with it no matter how big or small, because it is coming up for a reason. It is coming up so you can look at it. If you have done some inner child work before, you may have worked through this situation before. But it is coming up again because it is not complete. So, stay with it. I know there were several times when I had the same situation come up over and over, and it's frustrating as hell.

This happened because there were lots of layers that I needed to clear. My little six-year-old self was so angry that in spite of my tuning into her every day, several times a day, it took me about five years to peel off all the layers. It took me this long because she had been abused before. She was trafficked starting at the age of six months. If you are having a hard time soothing a part of you, there may be layers of earlier trauma that you haven't quite tapped into. You will tap into the darker areas when your mind is ready and not a moment sooner.

Trust this process and keep doing the work. It *will* pay off one day. Time is going to pass whether or not you do this work, so you might as well do it.

When the layers kept coming up, I felt helpless and angry. Many times, I just wanted to give up. I felt angry and even enraged at times at having to do the work. I believe that was my sense of entitlement. As if the spirit owed me something for doing my inner work. It felt like I was not making any progress even though I had all these realizations. I felt the whole thing was futile. How did I even get to the point of accumulating this much Karma? *If I stop now, I am still in the karmic cycle,* I thought. Then what was the alternative? Staying stuck where I was at was not an option.

I persevered and was eventually able to integrate my six-year-old self. Once I integrated her, then the next layer surfaced. You will find there are layers within layers of energy. During the time it took me to integrate her, I talked with my Higher Self about the possibility of moving forward without her. My Higher Self encouraged me to keep trying, and if we are not able to there is a way to leave her behind. But my Higher Self didn't want to take that route if we didn't have to because it would mean a whole huge cycle of reincarnation for little Simi as a separate entity, as she would have to learn all the lessons that I had already learned by going through the thousands of years of cycle of reincarnation. Integrating her was the quickest and most effective way to heal the fractured mind.

The next layer was the darker memories of being sold. Until I integrated the six-year-old, the other memories could not surface because it was too much, too dark, too soon. In fact, these darker memories surfaced just a couple of years ago.

The way to peel off a layer is to give your attention to a situation that pops into your mind. Allow it to take you deeper. Keep your focus on the ESS. I often found that something I thought to be a simple annoyance or frustration had a whole iceberg underneath it. The emotion was just a small, barely visible, scratch on the surface of that iceberg. Then ask yourself, *When was the first time I ever felt this way?* Once the situation has presented itself to you, then you will know the age when you first felt these emotions.

Once you know the age, in your mind's eye, travel back in time and space to when the situation occurred. When you arrive at the scene, observe what is happening. What is around you? What is the atmosphere like? How intense does it feel? Take a moment to breathe it all in. This will help you to deeply analyze the situation. When you are ready, freeze the situation. I would say freeze the situation right after the traumatic incident has occurred. This way you can heal the damage created by the trauma. This work within the mind's eye is the beginning stage of healing the way you relate to your inner child in whatever traumatic stages remain stagnant in your mind.

Acknowledge the younger version of you, and let them know that you can see them by saying hello. They may be surprised to see you. Let them know you are there to help them because you understand that life is hard. Let the smaller version of you also know who you are, that you are their adult self, that you have grown up. As you talk to them, watch their reaction to you. Do they like you? Are they glad you are there?

Ask if you can approach them. If so, walk closer. Then, ask if it is okay if you can pick them up or hug them. This will depend upon the age of the child. Feel into it and gauge what their needs and desires are. You will know exactly what they want because that is a younger version of you.

As you engage with this little one, you will notice that they are in fear. When you give them a choice, it alleviates their fear. So, at each point of the integration process, give them a choice. Again, ask them or *feel* what their needs are. Are they wanting to stay in the situation that they are in, or are they wanting to leave the situation? If they don't want to leave the situation, tell them that is okay and that you will come back.

They may not want to go back with you, or you may not want them to come with you because your present-day home doesn't feel safe to you, or you may not like where you live, so why would you bring a child into a toxic environment that you are not happy with? In this case, talk to someone who you trust and feel safe with. Ask them if you can bring your inner child to their home for a bit until you can integrate them. They just need to be aware of what you are doing. They don't need to do anything else. You don't need to move in with them. This way your inner child feels like he or she has permission to enter someone else's home. This will give them a sense of safety.

It really does takes a village to raise a child. This is why it is important to build a community of people who understand this work. When we reach out to a friend or a family member in this way it cultivates a sense of belonging within the child, and it helps the adult you to deepen your relationship with the person that you can trust to have this conversation with. You'd be surprised how your loved ones may respond to this request. When you can be vulnerable with your loved ones you give them permission to do the same. We need to have these deeper conversations if we are to build solid communities. Communities build the fabric of safety upon which we can thrive. Don't underestimate the power of vulnerability. It has the power to strengthen your bond and set a solid foundation for you to thrive. We don't have to be alone when we do this work. We need each other on this healing journey. Through this process you are beginning to build the secure attachment style with yourself.

As you embark on your journey of inner child work, your evolution will be noticeable by others, whether consciously or unconsciously. Remember, some relationships will fall away, while others will strengthen. Trust that whatever happens is to support you not to spite you.

If you happen to bring them to someone else's house other than yours, then go to this person's house, in your mind's eye, as frequently as you need to to integrate with this child. When you have integrated this child, you will be able to bring them into your current situation without causing further damage. You will also feel empowered to change your situation as well. Remember to always stay tuned in to the Voice.

The more you integrate your inner child, the better your life is going to get. This is an important part of the process. If you don't integrate with the inner child, your life may never change. Feel free to think of ways to coax your inner child to integrate with you. It's what we do as parents, and you are now their new parent.

When they are ready to leave the situation, visualize a white, serene bridge appearing in front of you. The bridge bridges the gap between the past and the present. As you cross the bridge together, you hold them and reassure them that all is okay. You can remind them that you are now older and have made it through life and you are okay. Life may not be where you wanted it to be, but you are still doing okay, you are no longer a part of that situation. Tell them that moving forward you need them in your life so you can live a better life. This will let them know that they are an important part of your life. Essentially you are telling your mind that you are important enough. When you get to the end of the bridge, visualize the whole situation and the bridge dissolving behind you as you step into the next chapter of your life.

When you get to the end of the bridge, that is the place where you will bring your inner child to. If you need to, reassure yourself and the little one that things are and will be different now that you are together. If as the adult you are having a hard time, then ask your Higher Self for help. You may have never connected with your Higher Self before, and that's okay. Trust that the support you need will be provided. When you ask for help, then be open to receiving it. Tell yourself that, "I am willing to receive help from my Higher Self." You will notice a shift and a change in you. You will begin to feel more at peace. You will have a sense of direction. Remember, you don't have to know how to do any of this. You just have to know that it will happen and trust.

Once you are home it is your job to make sure this inner child feels safe. Consistency breeds safety and trust. Show this little one around your house and introduce them to family members and friends. This is the beginning of helping your inner child to form a secure attachment with you.

This is a new relationship between you and your inner child. It will take time to form a bond and establish trust. Also remember this little one has been stuck in that one moment of time and space, and it thinks that he or she is still at the age when the trauma occurred. To get them off the hamster wheel of recurrent traumatic thought patterns, which are creating your reality, it is necessary to have a conversation with them.

Find a place where you two can sit and talk in private. Ask this little one to share their beliefs that were formed as a result of the trauma. Be ready to write down the beliefs this little one holds. They may tell you that they believe they are not good enough or important enough. Get as specific as possible. The more specific you can get, the quicker the energy will shift.

When you are done writing down their beliefs, then tell them to make themselves at home and get comfortable and that you will be back and take your leave. When you are by yourself, ask yourself, *How are these beliefs affecting my present-day life?* Look at all the situations that are going on in your life, and see how these beliefs are playing out in these situations. This simple act of awareness will shift the beliefs.

Over time, continue to establish a relationship with this little one. You do that by paying attention to your emotions. You will know that he or she is trying to get your attention by the way you feel. You will have the same emotion that you experienced that led you to him or her to begin with. This is their way of talking to you and letting you know they need help. When you feel that same emotion, tune into this little one and see what they need, or you can tell them that you will communicate with them sometime later. Make sure to make time in your day to talk to them if you want to make headway on this journey.

Once you establish trust, then your inner children will bring to surface all their emotions they had been holding back. They will let you know how they *really* feel about that situation, person, or place where the trauma originated. The adult you will feel the intensity of their emotions. This is why it is important to integrate one child at a time.

I was so hungry for this work that I found all of my inner children within one month. I don't recommend you do that because it can get very intense, as it did for me. Because now I was able to feel the emotions of *all* of my inner children *all* at once, and I hadn't quite learned how to release these emotions.

This work can get dangerous, so please use your discernment. Also know that energy can kill. An energy directed in a vicious way will kill before a bullet will. So, it is important to set your intention in a way so you don't harm anyone as you do this work. We are so powerful and can harm others simply with our thoughts. I set my intention in the following way before I began this work: "It is my intention to release that which no longer serves me by doing this work. It is my intention to heal myself by doing this work."

My sexually abused six-year-old self showed up early in the process. When I went to talk to her after our first meeting, she told me that she wanted to go to a beachfront. She was so angry that she wanted to stomp her feet on the ground and was afraid that in the process she might hurt herself, hence the beach. She wanted to go there at nighttime and have a bonfire going on the side.

Now I didn't live near a beach, nor did I want to go in search of one at night and build a bonfire. So, no matter what time of the day it was, I visualized our going to the beach, and it was nighttime. I visualized a bonfire by the beach. Then I sat there on the sand while she expressed her emotions. Whether it was by stomping her feet, screaming and yelling profanity, cursing, calling my mom names, the possibilities were endless. Then she wanted to visualize taking a knife and slicing our mother in half vertically. That gave her great satisfaction.

Emotions can only be processed and released though the emotional body. The dilemma is that we cannot have an emotional body without a physical body. These little parts of you do not have a physical body. So, any processing of emotions will have to happen through your physical body. To help her release her anger I, the adult me, needed to visualize killing my mom so I could process the emotions for this little child through my emotional body.

I allowed her to say whatever she needed to say. I allowed her to visualize whatever she needed to visualize so she could release this intense rage toward her mom. I allowed her to speak her mind unapologetically, uncensored. This was the only way out of the karmic predicament that I had found myself in.

It's because of the self-awareness of these thoughts I say that people who are intensely and severely abused, such as myself, end up in psych wards and correctional institutes, not in med schools. The only difference is they act on these thoughts, and I transmuted them. My psyche is no different than theirs. But my soul chose differently. It chose to release these thoughts instead of acting on them.

My six-year-old was animalistic and wild! There was no taming her. Sometimes I would sit there for hours witnessing her hysteria. Witnessing her screaming with her arms flailing and head thrashing about, I felt helpless and hopeless. How long was this going to last? How long would I have to put up with this discomfort? I guess it was going to last as long as it needed to. There was nothing I could do to speed up the process other than to simply be present, as frequently as possible, with compassion and understanding of how she arrived at where she was.

My karmic predicament was of my own creation. There is no one else to blame. Had I not slit my mother's throat in her previous life, she would not have abused me in this life. I could have potentially killed her in this lifetime again, keeping the karmic cycle alive. Instead, I chose to let the ball land in my court and not pick it back up. I chose to not volley. I chose to end this karmic nonsense. For me to do that, I still had to feel the rage that I felt because there was no suppressing it.

It took me years of witnessing these wildly enraged thoughts and actions of my six-year-old self before she finally came to the point of sadness. When the sadness begins you know you are getting closer to acceptance. For a couple of more years after I first experienced the sadness, there were waves of sadness followed by anger followed by more sadness. Again, I tuned into these tidal waves of emotions every chance I got throughout the day, for I knew that the only way out was to ride the tide that was going toward the shore.

There was a deep part of me that was unwilling to let go of the anger. It didn't matter that my life was in shambles because of the anger I carried toward my mother. I was unwilling to let it go until I journeyed with the magic mushrooms. They showed me what I had done to my mom in a previous lifetime. It was only then that I was able to let go of the anger toward her, but I couldn't look at my part until I had released the intense rage I had felt toward her. Upon seeing my part, I began to ask her for forgiveness. In my case, self-realization became a necessity. Enlightenment is not an accident; it happens when there is a necessity. Self-realization turned my fury into enlightenment. It enlightened my grieving heart. My enlightenment saved us both from pain and suffering caused by reincarnation. We both survived the turbulent seas without drowning each other in the waters of Karma. What a heartwarming gift the inner child work gave us, and only one person had to take the responsibility to do the work. I am not aware if she has taken responsibility for her part in all of this nor does it matter. Once I healed, I was able to separate our energies and can Love her like I would any other soul. Most souls on earth have *not* taken accountability for their actions. To me she is just another inhabitant of the earth. I am no more attached to her than I am to a stranger who is going about his or her journey, regardless of whether they have taken responsibility. I am not attached to whether or not she takes responsibility because it is not about her, it never was. One of my all-time favorite quotes is by Mother Theresa:

> "People are often unreasonable and self-centered, forgive them anyway.
>
> If you are kind people may accuse you of ulterior motives, be kind anyway.
>
> If you are honest people may cheat you, be honest anyway.
>
> If you are happy people may be jealous, be happy anyway.
>
> The good you do today may be forgotten tomorrow, do good anyway.
>
> Give the world the best you have and it may never be enough, give your best anyway.
>
> For you see, in the end, it is between you and God. It was never between you and them anyway."

My mother just became the impetus behind my journey to enlightenment. As we are all playing roles, she played hers beautifully. To expect her to take responsibility diminishes the whole point of this book. It is not about anyone but me. I am the one who went in search of the truth, she didn't. It was not a part of her journey. To expect her to make it a part of her journey is not honoring my own. Expecting that while writing this book and illuminating her not-so-kind acts, I believe, would be a great form of humiliation. It is not my intention to humiliate her in public, quite the contrary. By bringing her acts to light, I am helping her to liberate from her Karma and free her of the shame she may carry. For there is no shame in any of it because we are simply puppets of the ego until we embark on a conscious journey within. You and I are no different than her. The only difference is that you still have the veil of forgetfulness that is covering your not-so-aligned actions. Not to mention, I am being compelled by the Voice to share my story, and she happens to be a part of it.

It is wise to let go of the expectations of others, particularly in regard to remorse and owning up to wrongdoing. We are all on a journey that we signed up for before we incarnated. There are contracts that take place before we come into the physical form. It is not up so us to decide whether the other person should be remorseful or whether or not they should own up to their wrongdoing. If you think they should, then you might be waiting forever. For all you know, you may be the instigator of the karmic predicament you find yourself in with another person. So, who is to say who is in the wrong? Who is the judge of that? Who is to say who is wrong in a world where all we do is play roles? In a world where there are no absolute truths. In a world that is simply a hologram. This world is co-splay at its finest! If you still feel that the other person should take ownership, I feel that is a reflection of your not being willing to take ownership of your actions, for after all we are each other's mirror and 'as without, so within' applies here as well. This is your journey and yours alone.

When you begin the grief process is when you need to bring out your inner Buddha. Stay very present to all the emotions or the chatter that may arise. Stay nonreactive. Stay there as long as you need to. You don't need to sit in one place to do this work. You can be walking and become aware of the emotion that is within you. You can also be talking to someone and become aware of how you are feeling. All you need to do is simply be present to whatever is arising from within you.

Moving forward, you are your inner child's new parent. It is your job to connect with them on a daily basis several times a day. Initially you may start out connecting with them once or twice a day, but as you do this work you will notice the need to connect with them more often during the day. They will let you know that they want attention by way of feelings.

When you connect with them on a daily basis, ask them how their day was just as you would ask your biological child. If you are really tuned into them, they will let you know what they did or didn't like about the day. They will let you know if they didn't like someone and why. More often than not they are picking up on something you may have missed. They want to protect you. They have information that you may have missed. It's only when you integrate will you know what they want to reveal to you. They will make your life a lot easier in some ways.

Your inner children are your subconscious and the unconscious mind. When you integrate them certain things that were not in your conscious awareness will now become clear. This is how your intuition grows. It's these parts of you that have some information that may be of use to you. It's not to see your day through the lens of an inner child but rather to integrate what they have to say so that you have an integrated perspective on life rather than a split perspective.

The same principles of raising your biological child apply to raising your inner child. The Voice was my guide to raising my inner child. It even helped me to parent my biological children. The Voice knows information that is not only not written in books, but it will guide you through rough situations in ways that are customized to you.

There is a learning curve associated with this work. You will figure it out as you trudge through this journey and persevere. What better options do we have?

Find your Voice. It is waiting to be heard. This is a journey that begins and ends with the Voice of the heart.

When I first started doing this work, I would simply sit up in my bed, as soon as I woke up, and set my timer for five minutes and simply close my eyes. I would watch my breath go in and out without trying to change it. I observed how I had difficulty breathing at times. Other times it was an effortless flow. As I deepened my practice, I would ask a question that I wanted an answer to before I sat for meditation. I will share a few moments of my practice below to give you a glimpse of what it's like. This happened about four years into my work with the inner child. On this particular day I had asked for help with soothing my nine-year-old who was causing a rash on my leg.

A Walk Through Meditation

I had established the habit of sitting up in bed to meditate as soon as I woke up. This day was no different. I had recently moved to Colorado and had all the time in the world as I witnessed the ongoing war between my heart and the mind.

I sat up cross-legged in my bed as soon as I woke up in the morning. As I sat up, I adjusted the pillow so I could elevate my pelvis a bit. Once situated I simply closed my eyes. As I closed my eyes all the worries came rushing in, as if waiting for this window of opportunity to show themselves to me. I recognized the worries by the way I felt. I felt a tightness in my chest, and I chose to focus on my breath in spite of it. In that moment I was not aware of any worrisome thoughts. I kept my focus on my breath for as long as I could. Feeling its coolness as it entered my nose and feeling its warmth as it exited my nose. Soon I got distracted by thoughts of when am I going to find a job? Am I supposed to work? Or am I just supposed to sit here and do this inner work? And for how long? If I don't work, will I have enough money to survive? What will happen when I run out of money?

Then I remembered my breath again and began to focus on it. My nose began to feel itchy. I began to feel a bit restless. And oh, there comes a sigh. Wait, now I have the urge to straighten my back as I began to lean forward. Anything to distract me from sitting still. I just brought my attention back to my breath when I could remember it. I remained nonreactive for the most part, except for when my body was beginning to hunch forward. I gently brought it back to upright position again and continued to watch my breath the best I could. Soon, a sense of peace began to overcome me. And breath began to flow in and out with ease. This was my cue that the mind was quiet enough.

Suddenly, the Voice told me to bring awareness to my ESS, which was beginning to feel tight again. As I paid attention to the tightness in my chest, I felt the anger arising. The Voice was helping me to remember to bring awareness to my ESS so I could connect to the anger and its vibration. This anger was

159

coming from my nine-year-old self because she wanted my attention. When I tuned into this anger, I noticed that this nine-year-old was feeling angry by the thought of not being allowed to play badminton with her abusive cousins. She was reliving that moment over and over. She was reliving that feeling of rejection over and over. As I tuned into this anger, my mind was able to translate the emotions and feelings into thoughts. My thoughts matched my emotions. This is how I know that these thoughts were coming from the ESS. When I became aware of my nine-year-old self and held space for her to vent without judging her, the tightness in my chest dissipated, along with the anger of my nine-year-old self, and she stopped scratching my leg from the inside. This took about fifteen minutes in this particular round. I felt at peace the rest of the day, and my rash began to heal.

Chapter 10

Yoga of Relationships

*T*HE TOPIC OF RELATIONSHIPS IS a complex and a sensitive one. I can write a few books on relationships because they are all around us. Here I will address intimate relationships, because done with the right intention, these relationships will strengthen the relationship we have with ourselves. The most important relationship is the one we have with ourselves. When you right the relationship you have with yourself, you will attract abundance like moths to flame. When we have a healthy relationship with ourselves, we use that as a template to have a relationship with everything around us, including finances, food, animals, plants, etc. When we have a dysfunctional relationship with ourselves, we use *that* as a template to have a relationship with everything around us. It is up to us what kind of relationships we want to have. We are the key. How we treat ourselves is how we treat others and how others treat us. This is why I have dedicated my life to righting the relationship I have with myself. And inner child work has brought me to this stage of my journey where I can Love myself and Self. I can Love all of me, not just a few chosen parts of me. Sometimes, to get to that place of self-Love we need help from others. This is where intimate relationships come in handy. We need to experience the contrast so that we can see how we treat ourselves and learn how we want to be treated by ourselves. Because others treat us the way we treat ourselves.

During the first seven years of my journey with the inner child, I was alone and isolated. I lived alone in a glorified cave, which are known as apartments and homes in our modern times. It's not that I didn't want to hang out with others, it just simply didn't happen. No one contacted me, and I didn't have the desire to contact anyone. I was engrossed in my healing process. I was so focused on my healing that I made room to do this work by leaving my career, family, and friends, and liquidating my IRAs in preparation for this journey. This is the path of renunciation. In doing so, it gave me the much-needed time to heal. So, I could free myself of my mental prison. I would say 95 percent of my time was dedicated to my healing. The other 5 percent was dedicated to work and other household chores. There was minimal to no socializing. At times, the tree outside my back window was my company and gave me hope that there was life outside my apartment. The geese in the back yard were my companions during this very difficult time. After seven long, grueling years of giving of myself and opening my heart, I was ready for the intensity that intimate relationships bring. I could not have reached the depth of the pain that I carried without intimate relationships. But the emotional pain was too much to bear. Hence, I did the inner child work in isolation initially. There was no way I could have handled the intensity of the pain of an intimate relationship on top of the emotional pain I was already in. Inner child work helped me to clear the top layer of the pain before I took a deeper dive.

The intimate relationships that I was guided to participate in after doing my inner work were temporary. I was told by the

Voice that certain men were being brought into my life for my greater growth. At the time I did not realize that there was emotional pain stored within my body that I could not access without the help of a partner. Needless to say, my first partner was a man who used women to fulfill his needs. He wanted nothing more and nothing less. It was painful for me to be with him because I felt used again. The childhood memories of being used and abused came flooding back as if it had all transpired just the day before. They are sitting at the surface waiting to be stirred. This partnership showed me that it was time for me to release the pain of being used. This affair lasted for a few short months.

As soon as this one ended, another gentleman was sent my way. He was also a narcissist and had the field figured out. The women that he chose, he made them his concubine. I was no different. He said he was separated from his wife, but she still lived in the same house with him because he could not just ask her to leave. He never wanted to elevate me to the status of his wife. He never wanted to introduce me to his family. He often contradicted himself, sometimes saying his family would not want to meet me. Other times he said it was him who didn't want to introduce me to his family. He wanted to keep our relationship a secret. He also wanted to fulfill his needs, as he put it. I never knew where I stood with him. It was a very confusing relationship. This is the hallmark of a narcissistic relationship.

He had a budget of $100 per day to spend on a woman that he was with at any given moment. We would forgo dinner if we overspent during the day. He would instead bring up as much fruit as he could from the hotel lobby just so he didn't have to spend more money on food for the day. If I were hungry and he had spent his $100 for the day, I was on my own as far as buying food. As he lived out of state, he came to visit me for a weekend. After a weekend with him I saw him for who he was and wrote him a long email as to why I didn't want to be with him and how he was such a narcissist. I didn't care what the Voice had to say as I hit the send button. I was already feeling so degraded and unworthy that I could not bear to be with this man any longer. I didn't care what the Voice wanted in that moment. I just wanted to be done with this relationship. But the Voice found a way to get its message across to me. The Voice spoke to me through a friend who got in touch with me. She is the one who called me up and asked me what was going on. She shared with me that she was guided to reason with me. She conveyed the message of my Voice to me and told me that I needed to continue with the relationship with this man. If I didn't, then the spirit will find another man just like him for me, and it would take much longer. The choice was mine as to whether I wanted to learn the lessons now or later. I realized that once you commit to this path, the path will commit to you. Even when I ignored the Voice, it found a way to talk to me because it was an important step in my journey.

After reflecting on what my friend had to say, I decided to date this man for as long as I needed to, in spite of how humiliated I felt when I was with him. I wrote him another email apologizing for my behavior. I dated this man on and off for two years so I could release the pain that came with being with someone like him. Being with someone who thought the value of being with me was $100 per day at best. The irony was that he saw nothing wrong with what he was saying or doing.

During the two-year dating period I confronted him one day about how he makes me feel like a prostitute. When I confronted him with how I felt, he said the cost of a prostitute for someone my age was $50 per day, implying he was paying way more than what I was worth. It truly shocked me when I read that in the text. Such a callous, cold-hearted man, who didn't bat an eye while degrading and being condescending to a woman he was with.

But I can't say that I blame him for this. What he was showing me was this is how lowly I thought of myself. He was simply reflecting my thoughts back to me. This was my value in his eyes because this was my value in my eyes. He could not have treated me better than how I treated myself or how I thought about myself. He helped me to see where I needed to do more work. His degradation was my ammunition to Love myself. I felt the deep pain that I had allowed this man to inflict on me so I could release it. I allowed the tears to flow when he couldn't see me. For I didn't want him to know how deeply he had hurt me. This experience taught me the purpose of intimate relationships.

Relationships are meant for growth. They should be used for that purpose. This last man was certainly far from my prince charming. However, he helped me to realize that I am my own prince charming. That if I don't treat myself well, if I don't value myself, no one else can or will do it for me. People will treat you the way you treat yourself. Relationships are simply mirrors for self-reflection. Once again, this brings me back to the saying, "As without, so within."

We all want to be in an intimate relationship because oh, it makes us feel so good. I know I wanted to be in an intimate relationship because I felt so lowly about myself that I wanted that external validation that I am good enough, that I am worthy enough, so that I could give myself the permission to feel good about myself. But I had it all backward. I wanted a partner to help me feel good about myself. But the universe says that when you feel good about yourself, only then will you manifest a partner who treats you well.

There is nothing like an intimate relationship to bring your deep hidden pain to the surface. Excuse my crude language, but we tend to think that intimate relationships are for romanticizing and fucking only. While they serve that purpose, that is not the end-all, be-all of intimate relationships. That is just the icing on the cake of intimate relationships.

We tend to have erroneous fantasy about what it would be like to be in a healthy intimate relationship. But this inner world of fantasy cannot meet the outer world of reality unless you have first healed your attachment wounds. That's when we get disappointed and feel as if we have failed. When we approach relationship from a point of fantasy, we set ourselves up for failure even before we begin. Most of us have no clue as to what it means to be in a relationship and why they want to be in one. Unfortunately, they want it for all the wrong reasons.

Other than having healthy intimate relationships, why is it important to heal your attachment wounds, you may ask? There is a much bigger purpose behind them. Their main purpose is to help us to evolve. To help to unite us with our God-Self. They help us to realize God within us. The kind of relationship you have with your parents is the kind of relationship you will have with your God-Self, because your God-Self represents your parental figure in a lot of ways. Which means if you have an unhealthy relationship with your parents, whether they are dead or alive, you will have an unhealthy relationship with your God-Self, period.

Most of us go into intimate relationships without the knowledge of how dark it can get or having the tools of dealing with the deep pain of intimacy. Because we don't expect the pain to arise, we are caught off guard and tend to project the pain onto our partner. We hope that arguments don't arise. We look for the perfect match in search of that fantastic person who will complete us so that we can live happily forever after. The pain of an attachment wound is intense. It will pull the floor out from underneath you. It will shake you to your core. It is no child's play to deal with it. We need knowledge, tools, support, and compassion along the way. We need to be prepared to do the work. Make sure the timing is right for you before you jump into such a relationship.

Intimate relationships go through phases of pleasure and pain. You will initially feel pleasure by being with another person because relationships are meant to show you what it feels like to commune with your God-Self. As you experience pleasure with your partner you are forming an attachment with them. This attachment style is congruent with the attachment style you formed with your parents as a child. When I say parents here, I do mean your biological parents. This is regardless of whether or not you are adopted and regardless of whether your parents are still alive. The abandonment wound is still there for adopted adults, regardless of how good their adoptive parents were. The same is true if even if your parents are no longer alive.

While giving us pleasure, intimate relationships tend to bring out the worst in us like no other relationship. This is because the trauma that led to insecure attachment is stored in our womb space, regardless of whether you are a man or a woman. Men have an energetic womb space. When we have intercourse with someone, it shakes the energy of trauma and brings it to the surface. That's why having sex with someone tends to complicate things. It brings out the jealousy, the possessiveness, the neediness, the emotional avoidance, etc. This is the second phase of the relationships. It will show you what you need to clear to get to that place within yourself without the need for external support. Because that partner will leave you one day, one way or another. These relationships are meant to help us to release the pain of attachment wounds so that we can feel that joy and pleasure at all times, regardless of whether or not we are with a partner. So that we can form a secure attachment with our God-Self. This is what is called the Yoga of Relationships.

We fail at intimate relationships so miserably because we don't understand the purpose of these relationships. It's not about just friction of rubbing one part against another, as Ram Dass would say. It is about looking at oneself with a microscopic eye. It is about clearing and releasing your deeply dysfunctional patterns. It is about facing your deepest, darkest secrets, acknowledging them, and accepting them. It is about radical self-acceptance.

Being in an intimate relationship can be the quickest way to evolve if you allow it take its course. It can also be the longest way to evolve if you don't listen to the guidance when it is time to leave. Relationships can slow you down just as much as they can speed up your growth.

In my case, the Voice told me to not get involved with my ex. It told me to not to date him, let alone run away like I did, but I didn't listen, nor did I have the bandwidth or the courage to listen. I know we are ready when we're ready. But I don't think the Voice would have told me to not get involved if I wasn't ready at some level to hear its message. There is wisdom in the Voice, and we have free will. It's our free will, when it's not aligned with the divine will, that causes prolonged suffering and pain.

The consequences of me exercising my free will have rippled out to my future generations, starting with my daughters. It caused us to separate from our family, our culture, our community, our values, virtues, and heritage. Things that enrich our lives and bring joy to our soul, I stole from my kids. I ripped them off like a Band-Aid more than thirty years ago, and the bleeding has not stopped because the domino effect of my one seemingly small action is still in motion, or so it feels. For this my heart still aches, for the pain of separation is profound, leaving us in a state of destitution at times. Something feels lost and amiss. It feels like there is a hole that cannot be filled no matter how spiritually evolved I become or how enlightened I am. Because this is the ache of the heart, not the mind. I have a sense that the Voice knew the grandiosity of not just the repercussions but also the ripple effects of the repercussions.

When the lessons are done and you continue to stay in a relationship, there will be more arguments and fights. My marriage was one twenty-year-long-fight. There was no growth in it for me. If you are not growing from a relationship, it is time to leave. If you want to grow and the other person is not willing to grow with you, then you are not compatible. If they say they are willing to grow with you, then make sure that they are not just giving you lip service, that their actions match their words. This means that they are willing to take responsibility for their part in a situation. That they are willing to take ownership. Because growth is a form of dance, in this case between two people, Your Voice will let you know.

In this yogic dance, we tend to confuse the presence of our partner with the presence of our God-Self and think that we can't live without our partner. Your partner is simply pointing the way to something that is omnipotent and omnipresent within you. By the same token, if they are bringing out the worst in you, this is your guidepost as to what you need to clear to commune with God within you. This is the process. It's a process of contraction and expansion. Your Voice will guide you to perfection. It will let you know when to stay and when to part ways. Your Voice is all-knowing. Make sure to listen to your Voice.

Don't be surprised if you are guided to let go of a relationship(s) that is not serving you or your path, or if you are guided to not get involved with someone to begin with. When you do this work there will be an ebb and flow in your relationships. Certain ones will be dissolved, while others will be strengthened. Which means people will come and go. They will come to help you to heal, and they will leave when the healing is complete. This process will help you to detach while forming healthy attachment to your God-Self. This doesn't mean you try to detach. Allow the process to do it for you. Because if you try to detach too soon, it can be detrimental to your mental health.

As you probably noticed, I was able to heal the relationship with my parents through intimate relationships that I was guided to have post my divorce. The more I worked to release the pain inflicted by my partners, the more I softened toward my parents. The key is to feel the pain as it arises. To simply get present to it, no matter how uncomfortable you feel. To not react to it. As I healed this deep pain, my partners never knew what I was going through. Nor did I share with them. The more I released, the less angry I felt when I thought about my parents. Throughout this time, I allowed the Voice to guide me as to whether I should speak with my parents or not. There were long periods of time when I didn't call or get in touch with my parents, and they didn't get in touch with me either.

Then there were periods of time when we were closer. Again, go with the ebb and flow. There are no hard and fast rules.

I am unable to share with you whether or not you should talk to your parents or not. Or whether you should let go of a certain someone, because it is not my place to do so. Your journey is as unique as you. It is not my place to come between you, your Voice, and your Higher Self. I can only share with you what I was guided to do in hopes that it serves as a reference point to the kind of hoops I had to jump through. I have no doubt that you will be guided perfectly by your Voice, just as I was guided by mine. Trust the Voice and know that you are in phenomenal hands.

Epilogue

$\mathcal{A}$s YOU HAVE WITNESSED, I have come to an understanding of why my early life unfolded the way it did. I have healed my trauma through my journey, and my parents and I have a beautiful relationship today. I have since called them out for what they have done, and it was very difficult for them to face what they had done. They listened as I talked for hours on end about how they mistreated me and how that has affected not just my life but my kids' lives as well, as they simply listened and said that they were willing to repent. Although they never admitted to doing any of the things that I spoke with them about.

This journey has allowed me to release attachments and expectations, which in turn helped me to understand that they are on their own journey. Now that I have healed myself, their journey has no bearing on mine. The accountability that you may be seeking is not yours to seek. It is for the Lords of Karma to decide on the next course of action based on all that has transpired in this lifetime. For those who still want accountability I ask you this, "When was the last time you became aware of your actions?" You may only cast stones if you have realized and have an awareness of your wrongdoings.

What I will say might surprise you. Because of all the work that I have done in this lifetime, I feel my parents will be rewarded for the lessons they delivered because of the good that came out of it, even though it was because of my hard work. Ultimately, all that matters is the outcome of all that has transpired. Once again, it can be very challenging to understand these concepts. The invitation is to drop into your heart and feel the truth behind my words. The karmic lessons are based on not just the pain they have caused but its outcome. My guess is that there is forgiveness in it for them as well. Remember, ultimately this world is an illusion, and we are just playing roles.

This has been my journey, and yours will be as unique as you. No two journeys will be the same. How your journey unfolds is dependent upon your soul's path and your destiny. As long as we have Karma, we are bound by fate. Yet when we clear our Karma, we can step into our destiny.

I trust that once you begin your journey you will find the tools that you need within you to keep deepening your practice. As you connect with your inner child you will be shown what Karma you need to clear. I share my journey as a reference point of what it can look like. I have faith that you are well-supported on your journey by your Higher Self. I can't imagine I am that special that I am the only one who is being supported on my journey. I leaned a while ago that I am not that special. Thank goodness for small discoveries.

I would love to assist you with your journey. I welcome you to join my Facebook community called "Raising the Inner Child." Within the group, you will find support as you embark on your voyage into self-discovery. Here we can have honest and vulnerable conversations, and I will be able to answer any questions you may have. It is my hope that my work will inspire the creation of physical communities as well that are based on the principles of self-Love through inner child work.

Reach out to learn how to join me in person and online for weekly live Q&A calls. To further support you on your journey, I have also created a podcast called "Raising the Inner Child." I would love for you to join our community where we can support and nurture our children and each other as we walk home, together.

About the Author

Born and raised in India, Dr. Simi is a trained Family Practice Physician. In 2012, she stumbled upon inner child work as she was seeking alternative ways to heal her PTSD resulting from intensely dark childhood trauma.

As she began to practice the inner child work, it not only helped her to transcend her narcissistic personality disorder, but it also gave her a deeper understanding of how to manifest health in every area of her life beyond her physical body.

Being a physician gave her the scientific background on the pathophysiology of a disease process in regard to the physical body. Raising the inner child has helped her to tap into the root causes of disease in her life, which includes an understanding of how past-life energies play a role in our present-day life.

Dr. Simi has an aptitude for blending the physical with the metaphysical and a finesse for bridging science with spirituality. She has a keen prowess for energetically aligning the past-life energies with current-day energies to bring about health. Dr. Simi invites you to join her on this epic endeavor.

Made in the USA
Monee, IL
08 August 2024

62977431R00111